D1504972

Free Speech

Current Issues

Other books in the Compact Research series include:

Drugs

Current Issues

Free Speech

by Laura K. Egendorf

Current Issues

ReferencePoint Press™

San Diego, CA

For more information, contact
ReferencePoint Press, Inc.
PO Box 27779
San Diego, CA 92198
www. ReferencePointPress.com

Picture credits:
AP/Wide World Photos, 12, 17
Steve Zmina, 34–37, 49–50, 64–67, 79–81

Series design:
Tamia Dowlatabadi

LIBRARY OF CONGRESS CATALOGING-IN-PUBLICATION DATA

Egendorf, Laura K., 1973–
  Free speech / by Laura K. Egendorf.
    p. cm. — (Compact research)
  Includes bibliographical references and index.
  ISBN-13: 978-1-60152-018-0 (hardback)
  ISBN-10: 1-60152-018-2 (hardback)
  1. Freedom of speech—United States—Juvenile literature. I. Title.

  KF4772.Z9E34 2008
  342.7308'53—dc22
                                                    2007018023

Contents

Foreword

As modern civilization continues to evolve, its ability to create, store, distribute, and access information expands exponentially. The explosion of information from all media continues to increase at a phenomenal rate. By 2020 some experts predict the worldwide information base will double every 73 days. While access to diverse sources of information and perspectives is paramount to any democratic society, information alone cannot help people gain knowledge and understanding. Information must be organized and presented clearly and succinctly in order to be understood. The challenge in the digital age becomes not the creation of information, but how best to sort, organize, enhance, and present information.

ReferencePoint Press developed the *Compact Research* series with this challenge of the information age in mind. More than any other subject area today, researching current events can yield vast, diverse, and unqualified information that can be intimidating and overwhelming for even the most advanced and motivated researcher. The *Compact Research* series offers a compact, relevant, intelligent, and conveniently organized collection of information covering a variety of current and controversial topics ranging from illegal immigration to marijuana.

The series focuses on three types of information: objective single-author narratives, opinion-based primary source quotations, and facts and statistics. The clearly written objective narratives provide context and reliable background information. Primary source quotes are carefully selected and cited, exposing the reader to differing points of view. And facts and statistics sections aid the reader in evaluating perspectives. Presenting these key types of information creates a richer, more balanced learning experience.

For better understanding and convenience, the series enhances information by organizing it into narrower topics and adding design features that make it easy for a reader to identify desired content. For example, in *Compact Research: Illegal Immigration*, a chapter covering the economic impact of illegal immigration has an objective narrative explaining the various ways the economy is impacted, a balanced section of numerous primary source quotes on the topic, followed by facts and full-color illustrations to encourage evaluation of contrasting perspectives.

The ancient Roman philosopher Lucius Annaeus Seneca wrote, "It is quality rather than quantity that matters." More than just a collection of content, the *Compact Research* series is simply committed to creating, finding, organizing, and presenting the most relevant and appropriate amount of information on a current topic in a user-friendly style that invites, intrigues, and fosters understanding.

Free Speech at a Glance

Pornography

The Supreme Court has ruled that pornography is protected free speech if it cannot be deemed obscene. Many people believe that all pornography should be censored.

Movie Ratings

Movies released in the United States have been reviewed by a ratings board since 1968. Some people argue that these ratings lead to self-censorship by writers and directors.

Free Speech Zones

Placing protesters in restricted areas is a common occurrence at political events. Critics charge that these zones violate Americans' right to dissent.

Patriot Act

Section 215 of the Patriot Act allows law enforcement authorities to review bookstore purchases and library records. This section has led to debate over whether it stymies the ability of people to read and write freely.

Internet Filters

More than 90 percent of the public libraries in the United States restrict access to the Internet, most commonly by using Internet filters. These filters are intended to keep minors from viewing pornographic sites, but they may also block important information on topics such as breast cancer.

Television Censorship

The Federal Communications Commission (FCC) sets the standards on what material can be shown on broadcast television. Concern has arisen over whether the FCC is too quick to listen to the concerns of a vocal minority.

Speech Codes

Hundreds of college campuses have established codes that penalize students and faculty who harass others through oral and written speech. Critics charge that these codes violate First Amendment rights and prevent the exchange of different ideas.

National Endowment for the Arts (NEA)

The NEA received over $124 million from the government to fund art in 2007. Many people believe that it should not receive any government money because it sponsors artists who create works offensive to some.

Overview

The freedoms guaranteed by the First Amendment are the oldest of Americans' rights. While free speech has been an important part of American society for over 200 years, it has never been limitless. The government has placed restrictions on free speech from almost the very beginning, such as defining certain speech as being dangerous to national security, obscene, or libelous. While many proponents of free speech contend that the government is too prone to censorship, others contend that the U.S. government and court system have defined free speech too broadly.

Should All Speech Be Protected?

The First Amendment is not intended to protect all speech. The Supreme Court has frequently ruled that certain limits on speech are acceptable. For example, speech that might incite violence is not allowed; nor is obscene speech. The amendment also does not necessarily protect speech in private environments. For example, employees can be fired for comments made at work; however, employers cannot terminate workers for expressing their religious beliefs.

Speech that can undermine national security has also faced censorship throughout American history. During America's various wars, laws have been passed that censored newspapers or allowed mail to be read by government officials. These restrictions are intended in part to keep sensitive military information from reaching America's enemies.

Hate Speech

Hate speech is a type of discourse that the Supreme Court has debated on several occasions. In the seminal cases *National Socialist Party v. Skokie* and *R.A.V. v. City of St. Paul*, the justices ruled that communities cannot ban speech simply because they disagree with the message. They have also decided that controversial acts such as flag burning and cross burning can be protected under the First Amendment.

Speech codes are another way that society deals with hate speech. These codes have been established at hundreds of college campuses. While the content of the codes varies widely, in general the codes forbid students and faculty from saying or writing statements that can be construed as sexist, racist, or otherwise prejudiced. The intent of these codes is to protect women and minorities from harassment that may make them afraid to speak their minds. However, critics of the codes charge, these rules prevent a free flow of discussion and in some ways victimize the people they are intended to protect. They assert that the best response to hate speech is not censorship but more speech. Their belief is that it is better to respond to bigotry than to let hateful views hide underground. Nadine Strossen, the president of the American Civil Liberties Union, has stated: "Accordingly, the appropriate response to hate speech is not to censor it, but to answer it. This counterspeech strategy is better than censorship not only in principled terms—and consistent with free speech values—but also in pragmatic terms—and consistent with equality values. That is because of the potentially empowering experience of responding to hate speech with counterspeech."[1]

> " Hate speech is a type of discourse that the Supreme Court has debated on several occasions. "

The debate over how to respond to hateful speech received national attention in April 2007. Don Imus, a radio talk show host known for often controversial comments, referred to the Rutger University's women's basketball team as "nappy-headed hos." Imus's employer, CBS, initially

Radio shock jock Don Imus (left) meets with the Reverend Al Sharpton (right) on his morning talk show. The previous week Imus made controversial remarks about African American players on the Rutgers women's basketball team. He appeared on Sharpton's show to address those remarks and to apologize for offending anyone. Imus was later fired from CBS for the remarks. He has since hired an attorney who specializes in First Amendment law.

suspended the "shock jock," but then fired him a little more than a week after his comments. Although the firing was largely applauded, some people felt that suspension was a more appropriate punishment, particularly because the Rutgers team accepted Imus's apology.

Obscene Speech

The Supreme Court has distinguished between indecent speech, which is protected under the First Amendment, and obscenity, which is not. As long as pornographic material cannot be defined as obscene, adults have the right to write and possess it. In its *Miller v. California* decision the

Court devised a set of standards by which people can determine whether something is obscene. A key part of that process is whether the material meets community standards.

Many people worry that the court system is too liberal in its approach to obscenity and pornography. Organizations such as Concerned Women for America and the Family Research Council are particularly vocal in their concerns. They contend that local communities need to do more to keep pornography out of stores and off Web sites. Jonah Goldberg, the editor at large for *National Review Online*, echoes these beliefs when he writes, "Vile obscenity is a testament to the beauty of free expression, but free democratic debate is to be censored. Free speech in America is rotting from the inside out."[2]

Free Speech Rights of Students

The First Amendment is intended to protect all Americans, not just adults. However, limits have been placed on the free speech rights of minors; for example, they are too young to attend the showings of some movies. The free speech rights of students have been of frequent interest to the Supreme Court. In its landmark decision *Tinker v. Des Moines School District* (1969) decision the Supreme Court declared that students have the right to speak out on political issues on school grounds as long as their speech is not disruptive. The court system has also ruled on the right of students to publish controversial material in school newspapers. That right was limited by the decision in *Hazelwood School District v. Kuhlmeier* (1988), in which the Supreme Court asserted that school officials can censor school-sponsored newspapers without violating their students' First Amendment rights.

Students are often unaware or unappreciative of their free speech rights. A 2005 survey found that one-third of high school students believe the First Amendment goes too far in guaranteeing free speech rights. Half of the respondents also believe that government approval of newspaper stories is necessary. School newspapers are one way that students can learn about free speech, but more and more schools are eliminating journalism classes from their curricula. Kathleen Klink laments the disappearing school newspaper and the increased levels of censorship. She writes, "A journalism class constrained by a principal or superintendent might as well not exist. To control stories is to control free thought and free speech. However, to provide a framework built around a culture based on trust opens the door for students to explore ideas."[3]

However, in the opinion of Kevin W. Saunders, minors are not entitled to the same level of free speech as adults. He contends that unrestrained speech may be too damaging to the developing minds of children. According to Saunders, minors' access to violent or profane writings and songs needs to be limited so society can effectively teach morals. He explains:

> Society may have a right to make people morally better, but it has the period of minority to do so. Children must be trained, morally as well as in other areas. They need to be made into the morally best people they can be, but the project should be relatively complete by the time the child reaches the age of majority. To carry it on beyond that age is disrespectful of the equality of the individual. To engage in the task before the age of majority is to recognize that children are, in fact, not equals, in a sense, and that they need help in their development. The acceptance of a strong First Amendment for adults and a weaker First Amendment for children would allow society to protect children's best interests as well as its own.[4]

Libel and Slander

Freedom of speech does not mean that a person can say whatever he or she wants about another person. The First Amendment does not include oral or written defamation, known respectively as slander and libel. Such an omission is not surprising, because libel laws existed in England and the colonies.

A chief issue with defamation is that it can be extraordinarily difficult to prove. A person who is suing an alleged defamer must meet several standards, including proving that the statements were false and that they caused damage or injury. One of the most famous libel cases involved talk show host Oprah Winfrey. Texas ranchers sued her in 1998 after she made comments linking hamburger to mad cow disease. The jury ruled in favor of Winfrey in what many people viewed as a victory for free speech.

Another concern is that the fear of being sued can keep people from speaking critically about others, especially about those in positions of power. The Supreme Court has addressed this issue. In *New York Times Co. v. Sullivan* (1964) the Court ruled that public figures and officials must prove that the statements showed actual malice. The case involved an advertisement published in the *New York Times* that detailed the behavior of the Montgomery, Alabama, police department toward civil rights protesters. Some of the details were inaccurate, and the police commissioner, L.B. Sullivan, contended that these inaccuracies defamed him. The Court ruled in favor of the newspaper.

Limits on Political Speech

The right to free speech contains within it the right to speak out against the government. However, political speech has experienced restrictions. Placing limits on political dissent can be considered a particularly powerful form of censorship, as it can be seen as an indication that the government wants to limit criticism toward its policies. These limits are particularly prevalent in nondemocratic nations, but the United States has also controlled political speech at times.

Censorship of political speech can be justified in times when national security is the utmost priority. A government will understandably want to limit speech that may undermine its military or provide important information to its enemies. Finding the right balance between free speech and national security is a challenge. Civil liberties groups often charge that the government goes too far in the name of national security. On the other end of the political spectrum, some analysts believe that any criticism of the government may put the nation at risk. For many people, however, free speech and national security are not either/or propositions. In the opinion of Paul Rosenzweig, a senior legal research fellow for the Heritage Foundation, "achieving these goals is not a zero-sum game. We can achieve both—liberty and security—to an appreciable degree."[5]

Placing protesters in free speech zones is one way in which the government controls

> " **Placing limits on political dissent can be considered a particularly powerful form of censorship.** "

political speech. These zones are restricted areas, frequently at a considerable distance from the people whom the protesters are speaking about. Those who step outside the designated area are often arrested on charges of disorderly conduct. Government officials contend that these zones are a safety measure, but critics argue that these zones undermine free speech and create an environment in which politicians will only listen to people who agree with them. As Matt LeMieux, the executive director of the ACLU of Eastern Missouri, puts it, "Free speech rights are simply meaningless if they can only be exercised in an area far away from the intended audience."[6]

The Muhammad Cartoon Controversy

Political cartoons are often a target of censorship. Newspapers have repeatedly pulled cartoons on contentious issues such as terrorism and religion.

> " Newspapers have repeatedly pulled cartoons on contentious issues such as terrorism and religion. "

Such occurrences do not occur only in the United States. An international controversy emerged in February 2006, following the publication of cartoons in the Danish newspaper *Jyllands-Posten* that depicted Muhammad, the founder of Islam, as a terrorist. For example, one cartoon showed Muhammad wearing a turban shaped like a bomb with a lit fuse. These cartoons sparked violence throughout the Muslim world, where more than 100 people died in riots and Danish and Norwegian embassies were set on fire.

The response to the cartoons met with as much criticism as the cartoons themselves. Jonah Goldberg commented sarcastically about the rioting and deaths in *National Review*. "In our culture, we don't put up with violence and arson in response to speech. We're a funny people that way."[7] Other people criticized the decision of American newspapers to not publish the cartoons, asserting that the U.S. media have been willing to print offensive and controversial material in the past and that they should have stood up for free speech instead of fearing reprisals by Muslim readers.

However, many people also contended that the eruption over the cartoons is not a sign that Islam and free speech are at odds. Ziauddin

Sardar, writing for the *New Statesman*, explains that freedom of expression is part of Islam. She argues that the issue was not with the right of people to express themselves but with the demonization of Muslims.

In early 2007 a Danish court ruled that the editors of *Jyllands-Posten* did not commit libel toward Muslims when they published the cartoons. That decision put an end to the legal issues surrounding the cartoons, but the repercussions will likely continue to be felt as newspapers throughout the world grapple with how to handle potentially offensive cartoons.

Free Speech During Wartime

The issue of balancing free speech with national security is especially contentious during times of war. Reporters are most affected by wartime censorship, as they are limited in their ability to fully cover a war. Censorship has been part of most wars; for example, President Lincoln banned the publication of anti-Union newspapers during the Civil War. The Vietnam War was an exception—journalists covering the conflict

Antiwar demonstrators carry fake coffins through Los Angeles on January 27, 2007, as part of a nationwide effort to end the war in Iraq. The American Civil Liberties Union says police spy on professors and students on behalf of the FBI. Others say the government and police further undermine protesters by drowning out their speeches with police helicopters or by requiring protesters to pay costly fees for the right to gather in a public area.

had nearly unfettered access to soldiers. It is widely believed that the images presented by television journalists turned American opinion against the war.

During the Gulf War, journalists who wanted access to U.S. troops were required to join a press pool. An escort had to be present at all interviews. During the Iraq War, journalists were able to get closer to the military by being embedded with a unit instead of traveling in a press pool. However, the military placed limits on what information the journalists could report.

Some journalists contend that they have the responsibility to report fully on the war and to not allow the government to censor their reports. However, others believe that the media may have too much power and that competition for viewers, readers, and listeners too often endangers members of the military and intrudes on the government's ability to defend national interests.

Impact of Patriot Act

American attitudes toward terrorism and national security changed permanently on September 11, 2001, after a series of terrorist attacks on the East Coast left 3,000 people dead. Less than two months after the attacks, Congress passed a series of laws intended to protect the United States from future terrorism. Known as the Patriot Act, these laws have been controversial since their inception.

> **Opponents of the Patriot Act ... suggest that the government could better protect its citizens by improving communication and data sharing among its various agencies.**

Proponents assert that the Patriot Act has made Americans safer, pointing to the fact that no terrorist attack has occurred in the United States since its passage. They contend that the act has helped destroy terrorist cells and stop deadly plots. However, its critics believe that the Patriot Act undermines free speech and other civil liberties. They point to provisions in the act that allow law enforcement to search library and bookstore records and that make it easier for the federal and state governments to wiretap phone conversations. Opponents of the Patriot Act also suggest that the government could better protect its citizens by improving communication and data sharing among its various agencies.

Equal Right to Free Speech?

One issue that has been raised by proponents of free speech is that the media are controlled by a few corporations, which makes it difficult for people with out-of-the-mainstream opinions to express their views. In June 2003 the Federal Communications Commission made it easier for media corporations to own a newspaper and television station in the same market and to own multiple television stations throughout the country. According to Sasha Polakow-Suransky, a contributing editor for the *American Prospect*, the number of independently owned television studios has fallen precipitously, from 25 in 1985 to only 5 in 2002. Consequently, he writes, consumers are losing access to information and debate relevant to their own communities, because national media conglomerates find local programming to be too expensive and impractical to carry.

However, former FCC chairman Michael K. Powell contends that there are 140 percent more media owners than in 1960. He further asserts that new technologies have made it easier for Americans to be exposed to different ideas. According to Powell, "Cable and the Internet explode the model for viewpoint diversity in the media. . . . Citizens have more choice and more control over what they hear, see, or read than at any other time in history."[8]

Should Art Be Censored?

Artists may create whatever works they desire, but that does not mean that those works will be available to an unrestricted audience. The government and different industries have established methods for controlling the content of art. Since 1968 the movie industry has used a ratings system to determine which movies can be viewed by people of all ages and which need to be restricted to older audiences. Television ratings are a way in which parents and guardians can determine which shows their children can view.

For some people television ratings are insufficient. Groups such as the Parents Television Council keep a close eye on what they see on television

> **Although the methods by which people express themselves have changed, the issues surrounding free speech and censorship have not.**

and send letters to the FCC when they believe a broadcast network has crossed the line into indecency. The FCC can then decide whether to fine the network that aired the material. Perhaps the most famous incident was at the 2004 Super Bowl, when pop singer Janet Jackson's breast was exposed briefly during the half-time show. That moment led to extensive debate over the content of television, as well as discussion over whether the FCC goes too far at times in its fines. Some people believe that fear of fines causes networks to censor themselves.

Ron Paul, a member of the House of Representatives from Texas, is a critic of the PTC and similar organizations. According to Paul:

> Proponents of using government authority to censor certain undesirable images and comments on the airwaves resort to the claim that the airways belong to all the people, and therefore it's the government's responsibility to protect them. The mistake of never having privatized the radio and TV airwaves does not justify ignoring the 1st Amendment mandate that "Congress shall make no law abridging freedom of speech."[9]

The Changing Nature of Free Speech

The Founding Fathers wrote and ratified the First Amendment at a time when the only forms of communication were the spoken and written word. Technology has now made it possible for a person to present his or her views to millions of people with the click of a mouse. Although the methods by which people express themselves have changed, the issues surrounding free speech and censorship have not. Those issues and controversies will continue to be debated for years to come.

Should Limits Be Placed on Free Speech?

The First Amendment

The First Amendment reads: "Congress shall make no laws . . . abridging the freedom of speech, or of the press." In fact, not all types of speech are protected under the First Amendment. The Supreme Court has long viewed words that are harmful or obscene as not falling under constitutional protection. Free speech is an important right, but it is also a limited one. Understanding why certain types of speech are not free is important to fully comprehending the role of censorship in modern society.

One type of speech that the government can censor is language that presents "a clear and present danger." In the unanimous ruling in the case of *Schenck v. United States* (1919), Supreme Court justice Oliver Wendell Holmes wrote that if the government can prove that words or actions present a real and imminent threat, then censorship is permissible. The case revolved around the conviction of Charles Schenck, a Socialist who urged opposition to the military draft. According to Holmes:

> The question in every case is whether the words used are used in such circumstances and are of such a nature as to create a clear and present danger that they will bring about the substantive evils that Congress has a right to prevent. It is a question of proximity and degree. When

a nation is at war many things that might be said in time of peace are such a hindrance to its effort that their utterance will not be endured so long as men fight and that no Court could regard them as protected by any constitutional right.[10]

One example of speech that can fall under the "clear and present danger" definition is sedition, which are words intended to incite rebellion against the government. The Constitution protects seditious words as long as they do not present such a danger. Similar to "clear and present danger" is the notion of "fighting words." As defined by the U.S. Supreme Court in *Chaplinsky v. New Hampshire* (1942), these are words "which by their very utterance inflict injury or tend to incite an immediate breach of the peace."[11]

Another type of speech that the First Amendment does not protect is defamation, or lies that harm a person's reputation. Libel is the written form of defamation, while slander is spoken defamation. Some people feel that defamation laws go too far. David L. Hudson Jr., an author on Constitutional issues and a scholar at the First Amendment Center, contends that the ease with which defamation suits can be filed undermines free speech. He writes, "Defamation suits can further important interests of those who have been victimized by malicious falsehoods. However, defamation suits can also threaten First Amendment values by chilling the free flow of information."[12]

> " People sometimes confuse indecent speech with obscene speech; the difference is that the Constitution protects the former but not the latter. "

Some types of speech may be offensive to only one person, who believes that he or she is being defamed. In other cases the speech may be offensive to a much larger group, as in the case of obscenity. People sometimes confuse indecent speech with obscene speech; the difference is that the Constitution protects the former but not the latter. The exception to this rule is indecent speech that is broadcast on television or radio, because minors are more likely to encounter speech in those media than in books or magazines. However, even restrictions on obscene speech must not prevent adults from having the right to make or hear such comments; the goal of such censorship must be limited solely to the protection of minors, according to the Supreme Court.

What Is Hate Speech?

Determining a universal definition of hate speech can be difficult, as what is offensive to one person may not be offensive to another. The Supreme Court has made the effort, with several rulings on hate speech. The first major ruling occurred in 1977 in *National Socialist Party v. Skokie.* The residents of Skokie, Illinois, had sought to block the National Socialist Party (a group of neo-Nazis) from marching in their streets. The Court denied their request, explaining that to do so would restrict the free speech rights of the marchers. In this case, speech—regardless of how hateful it might seem—could not be censored.

The 1992 decision in *R.A.V. v. City of St. Paul* concerned a law passed by that Minnesota city that prohibited people from placing objects such as a swastika or burning cross on public or private property. The Court ruled that such a law was unconstitutional because "the First Amendment does not permit [a government] to impose special prohibitions on those speakers who express views on disfavored subjects."[13]

The Court also addressed cross burnings in the 2003 case *Virginia v. Black.* The case concerned two cross burnings that occurred in Virginia in 1998. The perpetrators were convicted under a Virginia law that banned cross burning. The Supreme Court's ruling contained two decisions. First, the justices ruled 6-3 that states may ban the burning of crosses if the intent of the burning is to intimidate. They also ruled by a 7-2 vote that not every cross burning is an attempt at intimidation and that states cannot pass laws that treat all cross burnings as evidence of intimidation. This decision indicates that under certain circumstances, cross burnings are a form of hate speech that is not protected under the First Amendment.

Should Hate Speech Be Defended?

The Supreme Court has ruled repeatedly that hateful speech can be entitled to First Amendment protection. Many politicians and commenta-

> **The Supreme Court has ruled repeatedly that hateful speech can be entitled to First Amendment protection.**

tors feel that that is too great an extension of free speech rights and have sought to place limits on hate speech. One law is the Respect for America's Fallen Heroes Act, which Congress passed in May 2006. The law prohibits people from protesting within 300 feet of the entrance of a cemetery operated by the National Cemetery Administration from one hour before a funeral until one hour after. Congress passed the act in response to Fred Phelps, a Kansas minister who picketed the funerals of soldiers who died in Iraq. He and his supporters attended funerals and carried signs with messages declaring that God is punishing the United States for tolerating homosexuality.

The United States is not alone in banning certain controversial speech. Israel and countries throughout Europe punish people who deny that the Holocaust occurred. In Austria a person can face as much as 20 years in jail for such statements. Britain outlaws speech that incites racial hatred. The European Union has also banned the broadcasting of programs that are politically or religiously offensive.

These laws are not applauded universally. Gerard Alexander, a visiting scholar at the American Enterprise Institute, writes of Europe's limits on speech: "It is not clear why avoiding offense should be a top priority to begin with. But when it is, the most important consequence is likely to be the chilling not of racist speech, but of moderate and conservative thinking about major social problems."[14] The American Civil Liberties Union has also been largely critical of hate crime laws because of concerns that those laws would punish not only violent crimes but biased thoughts as well.

However, other Americans praise these laws, asserting that there is no need to encourage bigotry, especially in the United States, where racial discrimination and homophobia persist. They further contend that hate speech undermines free speech because its victims are often reluctant to speak out. As Richard Delgado, a law professor at the University of Pittsburgh, writes, "Hate speech is rarely an invitation to a conversation. More like a slap in the face, it reviles and silences."[15]

Campus Speech Codes

One of the most controversial types of censorship that emerged in the late twentieth century was campus speech codes. Although the codes vary from campus to campus, they largely bar students and professors from using language that attacks people because of their race, gender, creed, or sexual orientation. More than two-thirds of all university campuses place limits on speech. Criticism of speech codes comes from liberals as well as conservatives, as both sides contend that these codes prevent a free exchange of ideas and are applied inconsistently.

A central argument against speech codes is that they insulate students and thereby make them unfamiliar with the reality of speech in the outside world, where they are far less likely to be protected from words that might offend them. Such insulation is unfortunate, suggests Harvey Mansfield. Mansfield, a professor of government at Harvard University, writes in the magazine *Weekly Standard*, "A society of free speech needs lively exchange between the parties and not just loud voices from its eccentric fringe—and this is true, too, for universities. For lively exchange you need balance, as it is easy for a dominant majority to be unruffled by dissent when it is only from a token few."[16] The American Civil Liberties Union agrees with Mansfield, arguing that the best way to respond to offensive speech is with opposing speech.

Not surprisingly, these codes have not been free of problems. The University of Pennsylvania abolished its speech code in 1993 after a student was punished, but later exonerated, for shouting "water buffalo" at a group of African American women. The court system has not been supportive of speech codes, ruling that these policies either prohibit too much protected speech or are unclear as to which expressions are permissible. For example, in 1989 a federal district court ruled against the University of Michigan speech code, stating that the university could not establish a policy that prohibits speech with which it disagrees. In 2003 the president of Shippensburg University, a campus in

> " A central argument against speech codes is that they insulate students and thereby make them unfamiliar with the reality of speech in the outside world. "

the Pennsylvania State University system, was ordered by a U.S. district court to stop enforcing parts of the school's speech code. Court rulings such as this one have no bearing on private universities, which can ban any speech they choose.

Speech codes do have supporters. Richard Delgado and Jean Stefancic contend that racial insults demoralize their targets and reduce the ability of the victim to speak freely. They also argue that universities have an interest in teaching people to treat one another with respect. Eugene Volokh points out that there should be some control over speech in the classroom—instructors should reprimand students who insult or harass their classmates and by the same token, instructors should not belittle their students. However, while Volokh agrees that limits to free speech are needed at universities, he draws the line at speech codes.

Pornography and the First Amendment

For the most part, pornography is protected free speech. The exceptions are child pornography and pornography that crosses the line into obscenity. The question is: Who determines what is obscene? The Supreme Court has ruled on this subject frequently over the last century, though it has often had difficulty defining obscenity. In the case *Jacobellis v. Ohio* (1964) Justice Potter Stewart wrote famously of obscenity: "I know it when I see it."[17] However, in its 1973 decision *in Miller v. California*, a case that involved the distribution of sexually explicit material, the Court established a set of three guidelines for juries to use when determining whether material was obscene: They must decide whether the average person, applying community standards, would find that the work as a whole appeals to prurient interests; whether the work describes or depicts sexual conduct in a demonstrably offensive way; and whether the work as a whole lacks scientific, artistic, literary, or political value. Of these three guidelines, community standards cause the most debate, because what might be acceptable in one community might be considered pornographic in another.

Regardless of how it is defined, pornography is found readily on the Internet. According to Patrick A. Trueman, a senior legal counsel for the Family Research Council, more than 250 million pages of pornographic material are on the Internet. Trueman further notes that pornographic magazines are available at local convenience stores. He suggests that citizens who are dismayed about the amount of pornography available in their neighborhoods can take steps to encourage local store owners to remove pornographic magazines and videos, even if the Supreme Court has ruled that such material is protected free speech. In this way, people can serve as censors in their communities. Another option suggested by Trueman is to make sure that laws governing obscenity are enforced.

Child pornography does not have any free speech protections. The Supreme Court ruled in the 1982 case *New York v. Ferber* that even if the material does not meet the standards set forth in *Miller*, states can prohibit child pornography. Eight years later the court ruled in *Osborne v. Ohio* that states can punish the private possession and viewing of child pornography. The Child Pornography Prevention Act of 1996 also applies to pornography in which no minors are involved but which conveys the impression of child pornography.

> **More than 250 million pages of pornographic material are on the Internet.**

Many people assert that the Supreme Court supports pornography. Conservative activist Phyllis Schlafly, for example, contends, "For decades, pornographers have enjoyed better treatment by our courts than any other industry."[18] She argues that the Court issued nearly three dozen pro-pornography decisions between 1970 and 1996 and that it continues to treat obscenity as constitutionally protected.

Despite Schafly's claim, the Supreme Court has in fact offered opposing views on the tactics the federal government can take in controlling information and images found online. In *Ashcroft v. Free Speech Coalition* (2002) the Court struck down provisions of the Child Pornography Protection Act that expanded the definition of child pornography to encompass images of people who appeared to be underage. However, the Court did rule by an 8-1 decision in *Ashcroft vs. ACLU* (2002) that the "community standards" definition of pornography could be used to determine how material should be regulated online and that the Child Online Protection Act was constitutional.

Are Internet Filters Effective?

The prevalence of pornography on the Internet has led to the creation of Internet filters, software that can prevent people (particularly children) from accessing certain Web sites. Due to the passage of the Children's Internet Protection Act (CIPA), most schools and public libraries have installed filters. CIPA, passed by Congress in 2000, states that institutions cannot receive discounts on Internet access unless they use filtering software and monitor the Internet activities of minors.

> " Due to the passage of the Children's Internet Protection Act, . . . most schools and public libraries have installed filters. "

The American Library Association is a vocal opponent of CIPA. The association opposes filters because it believes that they are ineffective, block sites that contain useful and legal information, and do not enable children to learn how to use the Internet properly. These views are echoed by other critics of Internet filters. In their article "Just Give It to Me Straight: A Case Against Filtering the Internet" professors of education T.A. Callister Jr. and Nicholas C. Burbules present four arguments against Internet filters: Filtering software blocks legitimate sites but allows access to sites that should not be accessible; it prevents students from accessing important and relevant information; it does not allow the user to know what information he or she has been prevented from seeing; and it is not necessarily more effective than teacher supervision.

Limiting the access of students to the Internet can go beyond filters. Some schools are either banning the use of the Internet entirely or allowing students to visit only a handful of selected sites. According to Mary Ann Bell, an associate professor of library science at Sam Houston State University in Texas, self-censorship by schools is occurring throughout the United States. She contends that these actions violate the First Amendment rights of students. By removing informative, although potentially controversial, Internet sources students have a limited ability to read and learn about different points of view.

Proponents of Internet filters assert that they are an effective tool in keeping children away from adult material. They dispute the claim that filtering prevents access to sites about breast cancer and other health information and contend that any imperfections of filters are outweighed by their benefits. Supporting filters in the case of *U.S. vs. American Library Association*, a collection of conservative family organizations writes:

> Using filter technology on public library computers results in less than one percent overblocking of protected speech. Less than one percent is truly minimal compared to the enormous amounts of illegal material that are effectively blocked. This provides an important and substantial amount of protection to our nation's children against harmful exposure to graphic, sexually explicit images on the computer. [19]

Even critics of the filters' use in public venues, such as the American Civil Liberties Union, have noted that the software is perfectly acceptable when used by parents. Internet filters can be seen as a parallel to television ratings systems; giving parents the tools to help them decide what material their children should be exposed to is much different from having the government make that decision, in the view of the ACLU and other anticensorship organizations.

> **Internet filters can be seen as a parallel to television ratings systems.**

The Supreme Court upheld CIPA in the 2003 decision in *U.S. v. American Library Association.* According to the Court, the use of filtering software to block access to pornographic Web sites is not a violation of the First Amendment. Chief Justice William Rehnquist compared library computers to books. He wrote, "Because public libraries have traditionally excluded pornographic material from their other collections, Congress could reasonably impose a parallel limitation on its Internet assistance programs."[20] Rehnquist further observed that CIPA does not impinge on the First Amendment rights of adult library patrons, because they can ask the librarian to disable the filter or unblock access to a Web site. Based on that decision, Internet filters will likely remain part of the library landscape for years to come.

Primary Source Quotes*

Should Limits Be Placed on Free Speech?

"In the age of the Internet, it is laughingly easy for kids to view pornography online."

—Barbara Dafoe Whitehead, "Online Porn: How Do We Keep It from Our Kids?" *Commonweal*, October 21, 2005.

Whitehead is the codirector of the National Marriage Project and an author who writes frequently on issues concerning families and children.

....

"Filtering software too often blocks perfectly legitimate sites and often does not block the kinds of sites that it was intended to filter in the first place."

—T.A. Callister Jr. and Nicholas C. Burbules, "Just Give It to Me Straight: A Case Against Filtering the Internet," *Phi Delta Kappan*, May 2004.

Callister is the chair of the Department of Education at Whitman College in Walla Walla, Washington, and Burbules is a professor in the Department of Educational Policy Studies at the University of Illinois, Urbana-Champaign.

....

* Editor's Note: While the definition of a primary source can be narrowly or broadly defined, for the purposes of Compact Research, a primary source consists of: 1) results of original research presented by an organization or researcher; 2) eyewitness accounts of events, personal experience, or work experience; 3) first-person editorials offering pundits' opinions; 4) government officials presenting political plans and/or policies; 5) representatives of organizations presenting testimony or policy.

66 Because public libraries' use of Internet filtering software does not violate their patrons' First Amendment
rights, CIPA [Children's Internet Protection Act] does
not induce libraries to violate the Constitution. 99

—William Rehnquist, majority opinion, *United States v. American Library Association*, June 23, 2003.

Rehnquist was the chief justice of the United States from 1986 to 2005.

66 Hate speech is rarely an invitation to a conversation.
More like a slap in the face, it reviles and silences. 99

—Richard Delgado, "Hate Cannot Be Tolerated," *USA Today*, March 2, 2004.

Delgado is a law professor at the University of Pittsburgh.

66 Provocative expression . . . tends to be associated with
social, political, or ethnic minorities' striving to make
themselves heard. Those minorities will be at greatest
risk from speech-code enforcement. 99

—Gary Pavela, "Only Speech Codes Should Be Censored," *Chronicle of Higher Education*, December 1, 2006.

Pavela is the director of judicial programs at the University of Maryland at College Park.

66 [Harassing conduct] includes [commenting] in a de-
rogatory way about a particular person or group's
physical appearance or sexual orientation, or their
cultural origins, or religious beliefs. 99

—Excerpted from the University of Michigan speech code, which was struck down by a federal court in 1989.

66Who decides what is offensive and, moreover, what is offensive enough to be called 'hate speech?'99

—Jarrod F. Reich, "Hate Speech Online," www.firstamendmentcenter.org.

Reich is a contributing writer to the First Amendment Center.

66Our politicians need to understand that a truly inclusive agenda includes standing up against hate speech.99

—Joe Solmonese, "This Anti-Gay Epithet Should Be Beyond the Pale, but It's Not," *Huffington Post*, March 6, 2007.

Solmonese is the president of the Human Rights Campaign, the largest gay, lesbian, bisexual, and transgender civil rights organization in the United States.

66St. Paul's desire to communicate to minority groups that it does not condone the 'group hatred' of bias-motivated speech does not justify selectively silencing speech on the basis of its content.99

—Antonin Scalia, unanimous decision in *R.A.V. v. City of St. Paul*, June 22, 1992.

Scalia has been a justice on the U.S. Supreme Court since 1986.

Facts and Illustrations

Should Limits Be Placed on Free Speech?

- **Three hundred** American universities enacted speech codes between 1987 and 1992.

- The U.S. Department of Education estimated that **90 percent** of K–12 schools were using Internet filters in 2005.

- A report by the progressive policy research group Third Way found that only **3 percent** of the pornographic Web sites available on the Internet requested proof of age.

- Filtering software blocks up to **23.6 percent** of nonexplicit Web pages.

- A survey by Pew Research Center found that **73 percent** of adults are "very concerned" about children viewing obscene material on the Internet.

- A survey of **300** colleges by the Foundation for Individual Rights in Education concluded that **68 percent** prohibited speech that is protected under the First Amendment.

- According to a study conducted by the London School of Economics, **9 out of 10 children** between the ages of 8 and 16 have seen **pornography** on the Internet.

Health Sites Blocked by Internet Filters

This table shows how one of the unintended consequences of Internet filtering software is that it can block access to important health information. Opponents of mandatory Internet filters in public libraries consider this a serious problem.

Web Site	Purpose	Filtering Software That Blocks Site
www.afso.org	American Society for Suicide Prevention home page	CyberPatrol
www.plannedparenthood.org	Planned Parenthood home page	CyberPatrol, Symantec, Websense, SmartFilter
Breastcancer.about.com	Information about breast cancer	8e6
www.cdc.gov/diabetes	Information on diabetes from the Centers for Disease Control and Prevention	SmartFilter, Websense

Source: Kaiser Family Foundation, "See No Evil: How Internet Filters Block the Search for Online Health Information," December 10, 2002.

Colleges Limit Free Speech

The organization FIRE (Foundation for Individual Rights in Education) rated 334 colleges to determine the level of free speech each school allows. Their study found that only eight of the schools, or just over 2 percent, did not place any restrictions on the First Amendment rights of students and faculty. In this graph, red indicates a school that has at least one policy that places substantial restrictions on free speech; yellow is for schools with policies that either restrict narrow categories of speech or for policies that can be interpreted as suppressing free speech; and green is for schools that have no policies that impede free speech.

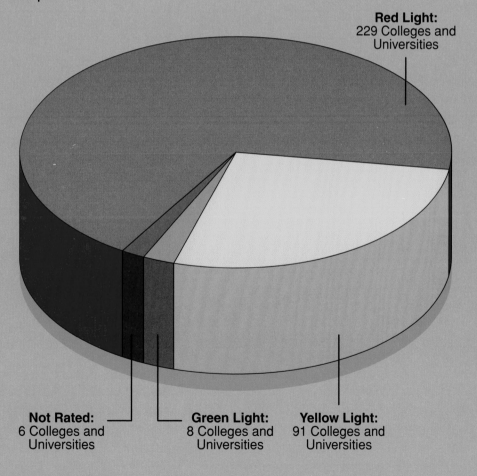

Red Light:
229 Colleges and Universities

Not Rated:
6 Colleges and Universities

Green Light:
8 Colleges and Universities

Yellow Light:
91 Colleges and Universities

Source: Foundation for Individual Rights in Education, "Spotlight on Speech Codes 2006," December 6, 2006.

- Only **11 percent** of the libraries that use filtering software confine the filters to the children's section.

Libraries and Local Standards

Should community members serve on public library materials-selection committees to ensure that local standards are considered for acquisitions?

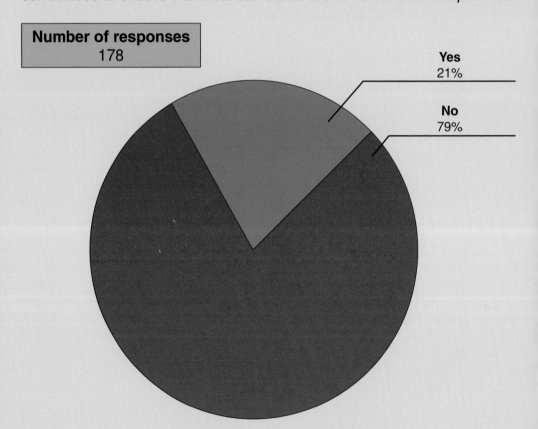

Number of responses
178

Yes
21%

No
79%

By a nearly four to one margin, librarians surveyed by the American Library Association believe that members of their local community should not participate in selecting materials for public libraries. This poll suggests that librarians feel that community involvement can lead to censorship under the guise of "community standards."

Source: American Library Association, 2006 ALA Direct Straw Poll Results.

Most Frequently Challenged Authors, 2003 to 2005

This table shows the 10 most challenged authors for 2003, 2004, and 2005. According to the American Library Association, a challenged author is one whose works are the target of removal or restriction. As this table indicates, some variation between the list occurs each year; however, some authors make continual appearances on the most challenged list. Books by authors on these lists that have been targeted include *The Chocolate War*, *Beloved*, and *Of Mice and Men*.

2003	2004	2005
1. Phyllis Reynolds Naylor	1. Phyllis Reynolds Naylor	1. Judy Blume
2. J.K. Rowling	2. Robert Cormier	2. Robert Cormier
3. Robert Cormier	3. Judy Blume	3. Chris Crutcher
4. Judy Blume	4. Toni Morrison	4. Robie Harris
5. Katherine Paterson	5. Chris Lynch	5. Phyllis Reynolds Naylor
6. John Steinbeck	6. Barbara Park	6. Toni Morrison
7. Walter Dean Myers	7. Gary Paulsen	7. J.D. Salinger
8. Robie Harris	8. Dav Pilkey	8. Lois Lowry
9. Stephen King	9. Maurice Sendak	9. Marilyn Reynolds
10. Louise Rennison	10. Sonya Sones	10. Sonya Sones

Source: American Library Association, "Challenged and Banned Books," 2007.

Should Speech Be Limited to Protect National Security?

Free Speech During Wartime

From the very beginning of American history, the U.S. government has placed restrictions on free speech rights during times of war. In 1798 Congress passed the Alien and Sedition Act, which made it a crime to publish "any false, scandalous and malicious writing" against the government. President Lincoln ordered the censorship of anti-Union newspapers during the Civil War. During World War I, Congress passed the Espionage Act of 1917. The act established the Federal Censorship Board and prohibited the writing or speaking of any words that might interfere with the draft or breed disloyalty.

Censorship during wartime continued throughout the 20th century, especially during World War II. The intention of these restrictions on free speech was to prevent sensitive military information from reaching the Axis governments of Germany, Italy, and Japan. The First War Powers Act, passed by Congress in 1941, gave President Franklin D. Roosevelt the authority to censor radio, cable, and mail. Congress also passed legislation that made it illegal for Americans to write anything that encouraged insubordination or disloyalty. In addition, Roosevelt established the Office of Censorship; the job of its employees was to examine public and private communications. A number of publications also voluntarily censored their contents.

Freedom of the press improved during the Vietnam War. According to Ryan Barber, the operations manager at the Oklahoma State University Library Publishing Center, military leaders decided that they could not restrict the movement of the American media because the U.S. government had never officially declared war. Reporters were able to speak with soldiers instead of relying on the commanders for news. Consequently, the media had more freedom to present images that turned Americans against the conflict.

> **Freedom of the press improved during the Vietnam War.**

The ability of journalists to cover wars to the best of their ability disappeared after Vietnam, reaching a nadir in the late 1980s and early 1990s. In 1989 the Pentagon permitted only 12 reporters to cover the invasion of Panama. During the Gulf War (1990 to 1991), the only foreign journalist allowed to stay in Baghdad was Peter Arnett, who was then subjected to censorship by Iraq. However, his fellow American journalists who stayed in Saudi Arabia were not much freer, as they were often constrained by the U.S. military.

Journalists who wanted to speak to the troops were required to be part of a press pool, and they could not conduct interviews without the presence of an escort. While these escorts were not censors, they did make coverage of the war difficult. As the Constitutional Rights Foundation explains, "Reporters protested that escorts intimidated soldiers being interviewed, sometimes even speaking for them. The media objected when the military kept pool reporters from visiting scenes where Americans had been killed. The press complained most often about delays in getting dispatches from the field through the military-review system."[21] Although wartime rules displeased the news media, 68 percent of Americans polled at that time believed that the level of military control was appropriate, with only 13 percent feeling that the media deserved more freedom of the press.

During the war in Iraq, more than 600 American journalists who wanted to cover the battles chose to be embedded with troops. This

> **Embedded journalists were able to offer a bird's-eye perspective on the war and more insight into the everyday life of U.S. soldiers.**

meant that they traveled with the troops rather than as part of a press pool. Restrictions remained, however; the military told journalists which information could not be broadcast, such as the specific location of troops and information about future military operations. Another consequence of embedding was that journalists became part of the story and often found it difficult to separate themselves emotionally and intellectually from the military. On the other hand, embedded journalists were able to offer a bird's-eye perspective on the war and more insight into the everyday life of U.S. soldiers.

Responsibilities of Journalists

Even if the government did not place restrictions on the freedom of speech and freedom of the press when the United States is at war, journalists would still have the responsibility to report the news in a way that does not pose a threat to soldiers. Debate has arisen over how journalists can do their jobs properly while not impinging on national security.

In an article in *Reason*, columnist Nat Hentoff is quoted as stating that journalists have the responsibility to report on war truthfully. He notes:

> In the Gulf War, the government managed to tie the hands of the press totally. In other words, practically no information came out except from the government. By contrast, in the much more dangerous Vietnam War, there was a great deal of free reporting and as a result of that, people began to understand what was going on and there were political changes.[22]

Truthfulness can be difficult to achieve, some critics of the news media believe. They view journalists as more than willing to support anything that the government does instead of questioning foreign policy decisions. Jack D. Douglas, a former professor of sociology at the University of California at San Diego, asserts that the media "have covered a wider spectrum of the public discourse before invasions and annihilations and vast war crimes, but they always have fallen in line and saluted once the firing starts."[23]

At the same time, some people complain that American journalists have too much freedom. In an interview with *National Review*, Egyptian-born writer Nonie Darwish compares Arab media, which are controlled by the government, with the Western media. In Darwish's view the relative lack of government control over American journalists is not necessarily positive, because the Western media's distaste for restrictions and their belief that freedom of the press supersedes national security can backfire and help America's enemies. For example, Western journalists might reveal too much information about military plans, and those details could be readily learned by opposing forces.

Free Speech vs. Security

Americans have often had to struggle with choosing between free speech and national security. The various censorship laws passed during wartime are evidence of that. In the 1950s during the height of the Red Scare and McCarthyism, writers and folk singers found themselves blacklisted and their political views placed under the microscope. Despite this history, however, U.S. society does not necessarily have to choose between freedom of speech or protecting its citizens.

Richard Posner, writing for the *Atlantic Monthly*, asserts that both needs can coexist. He writes that civil liberties are always important, even during times of war. At the same time, however, a balance needs to be struck. "Lincoln's unconstitutional acts during the Civil War show that even legality must sometimes be sacrificed for other values. We are a nation under law, but first we are a nation."[24]

> **Americans have often had to struggle with choosing between free speech and national security.**

However, the government may sometimes go too far in its effort to find a balance. In its report "Freedom Under Fire: Dissent in Post-9/11 America" the American Civil Liberties Union details some of the ways in which free speech has been undermined. The ACLU cites examples such as police assaulting protesters in Missouri and California and campus police spying on professors and students on behalf of the FBI. Lewis Lapham, the editor *of Harper's Weekly*, notes that the government and police further undermine protesters by drowning out their speeches with police helicopters or by requiring protesters to pay costly fees for the right to gather in a public area.

Free Speech Zones

Free speech zones are a recent and controversial addition to restrictions intended to protect national security. These zones place protesters in restricted areas, often at a considerable distance from the people whom they are protesting. People who step outside the designated area are often arrested on charges of disorderly conduct. These zones have become fixtures at political conventions and presidential appearances.

Government officials and police officers assert that free speech zones are necessary to protect people from injury; for example, preventing a protester from getting distracted and being hit by a car. Colleges have also adopted the use of free speech zones, with administrators also arguing that these designated areas are intended to prevent disrupting students on their way to class. Journalist Geoffrey Stone asserts that the idea of restricting free speech in order to protect people's safety, in particular the safety of the president, has merit. However, Stone observes, these zones should follow three basic conditions. First, the zone must be no farther away than is necessary to protect the president. Second, free speech zones should not be created as a way of protecting the president from criticism. Lastly, these zones should not apply only to people who are protesting the president and government; presidential supporters should also be obligated to speak within the free speech zone.

> " One of the major criticisms of free speech zones is that they are used solely to restrict the First Amendment rights of critics of the president or other politicians. "

It is the last requirement that is most often ignored. One of the major criticisms of free speech zones is that they are used solely to restrict the

First Amendment rights of critics of the president or other politicians (for example, these zones were used at the 2004 political conventions), while their supporters can get as close as the Secret Service allows. Opponents of free speech zones charge that the zones' use treats protesters as enemies rather than as U.S. citizens with full constitutional rights. In some cases the treatment of people who step outside the zones can become absurd. James Bovard cites an instance where a woman was arrested and separated from her five-year-old daughter, while Lapham details the arrest of an unemployed steel worker who was decrying President George W. Bush's economic policies.

Judges have reluctantly upheld the right of the government to establish free speech zones. They acknowledge that the zones are an affront to the First Amendment but rule that safety concerns must take precedence.

Is the First Amendment at Risk?

The U.S. government's often negative attitude toward free speech during wartime is worrisome to many people. Some analysts are particularly concerned that the media are not being as active as they could be in protecting the First Amendment and speculate that this reticence is out of fear of being viewed as disloyal or because they are afraid of offending the stockholders who support the major media corporations. However, according to Christopher B. Daly, a professor of journalism at Boston University, journalists must always be ready to defend the First Amendment. He states, "Whatever degree of freedom the press has is the result of a struggle, not a foreordained declaration. Every generation or so, Americans find they must renew this struggle to defend freedom of the press."[25]

One challenge that journalists face is the possibility of being charged under the Espionage Act of 1917. A district judge has ruled that the George W. Bush administration can use the act to bring criminal charges against journalists who spread leaked classified material. This decision may make government whistleblowers hesitant to contact the press, at a further cost to First Amendment rights.

However, these concerns may be overblown. The United States has been through numerous wars and other challenges to its security, but the First Amendment remains intact. Journalists face the same obstacles in each war. However, the press is unlikely to ever be fully controlled by the government. Laws may be passed that make it difficult to publish dissenting views, yet those laws are invariably overturned or end once the danger passes. For example, the Alien and Sedition Acts expired as soon as Thomas Jefferson took office.

> **The press is unlikely to ever be fully controlled by the government.**

Effects on Foreign Policy

The impact that free speech has on foreign policy is unclear. It may well be that government censorship is more dangerous than the speech it is seeking to control. At the same time, dissent can undermine national unity and cause distrust of the government and the military. Syndicated columnist Cal Thomas suggests, "Debate now merely emboldens our enemies, who see division as lack of resolve. Worse, it might demoralize our troops."[26]

The Constitution is the bulwark of American society, and the First Amendment is perhaps the best-known portion of the Constitution. Consequently, government infringement on the right of citizens to assemble and protest may well undermine the foundation of the country. However, in times of war and terrorism, the United States cannot automatically assume that assembly and protest are safe. Free speech and national security may have to coexist for years to come, with neither side's supporters ever being satisfied completely.

Should Speech Be Limited to Protect National Security?

66 **The proper response of the government should not be to prohibit dissent, but to protect the speaker and punish those who resort to violence.** 99

—Geoffrey Stone, interview by Ronald K.L. Collins, *First Amendment Center First Reports,* November 2004.

Stone is a professor at the University of Chicago Law School.

66 **Free speech rights are simply meaningless if they can only be exercised in an area far away from the intended audience.** 99

—Matt LeMieux, quoted in "Freedom Under Fire: Dissent in Post-9/11 America," American Civil Liberties Union, December 8, 2003.

LeMieux is the executive director of the ACLU of Eastern Missouri.

* Editor's Note: While the definition of a primary source can be narrowly or broadly defined, for the purposes of Compact Research, a primary source consists of: 1) results of original research presented by an organization or researcher; 2) eyewitness accounts of events, personal experience, or work experience; 3) first-person editorials offering pundits' opinions; 4) government officials presenting political plans and/or policies; 5) representatives of organizations presenting testimony or policy.

66 When assessing civil liberty questions, it is important not to lose sight of the underlying purpose of government: personal and national security. The balance between civil liberties and security is not a zero-sum game. 99

—The Heritage Foundation, *Heritage Special Report: The Patriot Act Reader*, September 20, 2004.

The Heritage Foundation is a think tank that supports limited government.

66 Debate now merely emboldens our enemies, who see division as lack of resolve. Worse, it might demoralize our troops. 99

—Cal Thomas, "Protest Votes," *USA Today*, February 7, 2007. www.usatoday.com.

Thomas is a syndicated columnist.

66 During wartime, you see, anyone who criticizes the government is a traitor, and any journalist with access to military intelligence a potential threat to national security. 99

—Cynthia Cotts, "War Means Never Having to Tell the Truth," *Village Voice*, September 26, 2001.

Cotts is the senior editor of the magazine *American Lawyer*.

66 Nowhere is it written that military personnel forfeit their First Amendment right to freedom of expression. 99

—Ted Galen Carpenter, "Free Speech for Generals," April 28, 2006. www.cato.org.

Carpenter is the vice president for defense and foreign policy studies at the Cato Institute, a libertarian policy research organization.

66 Embedding, too often, is a pact made with the devil, where the freedom to report on any aspect of what you are seeing is partially surrendered in exchange for access to the battlefield. 99

—Peter Beaumont, "Why Embedded Journalists Are Being Taken for a Ride," *Observer (London)*, November 21, 2004.

Beaumont is the foreign affairs editor for the *Observer*, a British newspaper.

Should Speech Be Limited to Protect National Security?

- Since 1997 approximately **250 journalists** have died covering wars and armed conflicts.

- The free speech zone that was used at the 2004 Democratic National Convention was large enough to hold **1,000 people**.

- According to a 2006 survey, **73.6 percent** of respondents received their news from local television; **68.9 percent** relied on their local newspaper.

- Coverage of the war on terrorism has been rated as important by **90 percent** of television and newspaper journalists.

- As of October 2006 approximately **two dozen** embedded reporters were in Iraq.

- The U.S. government abolished the **Office of Censorship** on November 15, 1945.

- A U.S. district judge has ruled that the George W. Bush administration can use the **Espionage Act of 1917** to prosecute American citizens who gain access to information about national defense.

- In 1798 Matthew Lyon, a congressman from Vermont, was the first person put on trial under the **Alien and Sedition Acts**; he was found guilty and sent to jail and fined.

Newspaper Criticism of Wartime Governments

Even during wartime, the press should be allowed to publish stories that criticize the actions of the government.

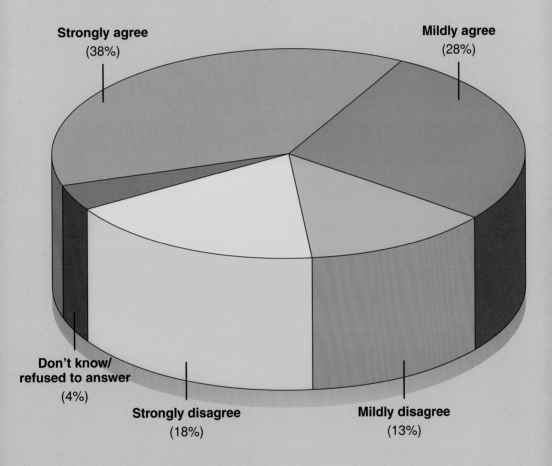

Strongly agree
(38%)

Mildly agree
(28%)

Don't know/
refused to answer
(4%)

Strongly disagree
(18%)

Mildly disagree
(13%)

*Numbers don't add to 100 due to rounding up.

In 2006, 66 percent of the people polled by the First Amendment Center agreed that the press has the right to criticize the government during wartime. This result indicates that freedom of the press is a popular idea, even at times when the government might use methods of wartime censorship.

Source: First Amendment Center, *2006 State of the First Amendment Survey*, November 11, 2006.

Television Coverage of Foreign Events Has Decreased

A study conducted by the Project for Excellence in Journalism found that the three major television networks have sharply decreased the number of reports coming from reporters stationed outside the United States. Although coverage increased in 2003, the first year of the war in Iraq, that increase did not last into the following years.

Year	ABC	CBS	NBC	Total 7 minutes of coverage
1988	1158	1090	1013	3257
1989	1397	1454	1181	4032
1990	1414	1377	1081	3872
1991	1417	1132	1217	3766
1992	1037	736	749	2521
1993	1057	752	543	2352
1994	992	974	768	2733
1995	784	740	467	1990
1996	577	692	327	1596
1997	609	666	356	1631
1998	513	647	304	1464
1999	654	687	457	1799
2000	481	479	422	1382
2001	588	628	451	1667
2002	667	779	657	2103
2003	848	1007	917	2772
2004	711	890	823	2424
2005	718	894	746	2358
2006	654	837	700	2191

Source: Project for Excellence in Journalism, "The State of the News Media 2007," 2007.

Should the Media Be Censored?

" [American citizens] want protection from smut yet don't use the V chip. They talk about competing with pop culture to parent their children yet give kids TVs and computers in their bedrooms. **"**

—James Poniewozik, "The Decency Police."

Artists often use their talents to express unpopular or controversial views, such as creating movies that criticize U.S. foreign policy or writing books depicting sexually active teenagers. However, at times artists find themselves facing censorship by the government and private citizens. Censorship of art can range from cities refusing to fund exhibits they find objectionable to school boards pulling books from library shelves to the Federal Communications Commission placing restrictions on speech on television and radio. Debate centers on whether artists are entitled to complete freedom or if they need to meet certain standards of decency.

Are Movie Ratings a Type of Censorship?

Prior to 1968, movies released in the United States were unrated. That is not to say, however, that producers, writers, and directors could create whatever type of movie they desired. Movies released between 1930 and 1968 were expected to hew to the Hays Code, a set of standards established by the movie industry that placed a number of restrictions on films, including barring them from showing certain crimes or sexual behaviors, among other restrictions. According to the Hays Code, these rules were necessary because "if motion pictures consistently hold up for admiration high types of characters and present stories that will affect lives for the better, they can become the most powerful force for the improvement of mankind."[27]

On November 1, 1968, the Hays Code was supplanted by the movie ratings system that is still in use today. Established by the Motion Picture Association of America (MPAA), movies were initially awarded one of four ratings: G, M, R, and X. Anyone, regardless of age, could attend G-rated movies. The M rating, which stood for "Mature," indicated a movie that was acceptable for all ages but for which parental guidance was suggested. In 1970 the M rating was replaced by GP, later termed PG. R-rated movies were initially prohibited to unaccompanied children under the age of 16, later raised to 17. No one under 17 was allowed to attend an X-rated movie. In 1990 the MPAA changed the X rating to NC-17. Another major change to the ratings system occurred in 1984, when the MPAA added the PG-13 rating for movies that were more intense than PG films but lacked the sexual or violent content of R-rated movies.

> " The movie ratings system is not meant to censor material but to inform parents of the contents of movies. "

The movie ratings system is not meant to censor material but to inform parents of the contents of movies so that they can determine whether a film is appropriate for their children to view. However, critics of the MPAA contend that the ratings are a de facto form of censorship because of the way in which the ratings are applied. One argument is that a movie with explicit sex will likely be rated NC-17, while a gory horror movie is more likely to receive an R rating; perhaps not coincidentally, violent films appeal to young men, an audience that is highly prized by the movie industry. Monetary considerations also lead movie studios to edit their films in order to earn a less restrictive rating and ensure a wider audience and higher profits. Many critics believe that this editing lessens the quality of films intended for more mature audiences.

A further problem, in the view of *Philadelphia Inquirer* movie critic Carrie Rickey, is that the MPAA is beholden to the movie studios whose films it rates. As she puts it, "The MPAA serves two masters. It is a trade and lobbying agency for the movie studios in Washington and the provider of ratings guidelines for consumers. Is it a conflict of interest when one arm of an organization represents a studio that wants a favorable rating that the organization's other arm might confer?"[28]

In response to concerns over how ratings are determined, the MPAA instituted several changes in January 2007. In the past, the people who sat on the ratings board remained anonymous. Now, the names of the three senior raters are posted on the association's Web site. Furthermore, directors who seek to appeal their films' ratings are able to cite similar scenes from other movies. A policy stating that raters must have school-age children will also be enforced.

Movie censorship can also occur when the film is released on DVD. One of the largest video rental chains, Blockbuster, will not carry NC-17 or X-rated movies, limiting the ability of adults to watch those films. Several companies remove potentially offensive material from films to make them more family friendly. The directors of these movies view this as a form of censorship that destroys their cinematic vision. Congress made such editing legal when it passed the Family Entertainment and Copyright Act in 2005. The act states that as long as there is a notice at the beginning of the film stating that there have been alterations, no copyright has been infringed.

Regulating Television Content

Concern over the content of television programs, particularly on cable television, prompted the industry to adopt a ratings system. In 1997 a system was established with ratings ranging from TV-Y (appropriate for all children) to TV-MA (may be inappropriate for children under 17 due to graphic sex and violence). Series are rated on an episode-by-episode basis rather than as a whole.

For parents who want greater control over what their children watch, the V-chip (the *v* stands for "violence") is a piece of technology available in all televisions built after 1999 that allows inappropriate material to be blocked, rather than censored. For example, a parent can block all programs rated TV-14 or higher. Programs can be unblocked for viewing by adults and older children. The V-chip and the ratings system allow parents to supervise their children's viewing habits. Rod Gustafson, writing for the

Parents Television Council (PTC), compares these approaches to food content labels—"advisories that allow busy families to carefully consider their entertainment choices and make informed consumer decisions."[29]

The Role of the Federal Communications Commission

At times the contents of a television show go beyond what some people consider acceptable. In response, they often turn to the Federal Communications Commission (FCC) in the hope of penalizing the network that aired the offensive material. Many people believe that the FCC is too quick to fine networks based on such protests and contend that television shows are opting for self-censorship because they fear becoming the target of protests.

> **Many people believe that the FCC is too quick to fine networks.**

The Parents Television Council is one of the leading organizations in that arena. It tracks the content of thousands of hours of television, noting the language, violence, and sexual content. The purpose of the PTC is "to ensure that children are not constantly assaulted by sex, violence and profanity on television and in other media."[30] The council states on its Web site that it does not censor television because it is merely providing information about the content of television programs, not preventing those programs from airing.

One of the most infamous incidents of indecency on television occurred at the 2004 Super Bowl half-time show, when pop singers Justin Timberlake and Janet Jackson performed a routine that culminated in Timberlake ripping off part of Jackson's shirt, revealing one of her breasts. Although the image was brief and not seen by all viewers, it led to a maelstrom over what material can be shown on commercial television. The FCC fined CBS, the network that broadcast the Super Bowl, $550,000. According to the commission, "The halftime show is patently offensive as measured by contemporary community standards for the broadcast medium. The commission determined that the broadcast of partial nudity in this instance was explicit and graphic and appeared to pander to, titillate and shock the viewing audience."[31]

One concern is that while only a handful of people protest the contents of a show, they affect the ability of millions of adults to watch programs of their own choosing. In an article in *Time*, James Poniewozik points out that although 159 letters of complaint were written about the show *Married by America*, only 23 different people wrote a letter, and 21 of them used a form letter.

The writers' organization PEN Center USA has been highly critical of the actions taken by the Parents Television Council. According to the center, networks are opting to censor shows rather than risk complaints. The Public Broadcasting System (PBS) removed swearing from a documentary about Iraq and excised a scene of a naked woman in a decontamination shower from a British show about a bombing in London. The center argues that networks must self-censor because "due to legality issues, the FCC cannot warn what is offensive or not beforehand."[32]

The government does have the right to censor television. As Poniewozik explains in the above-mentioned article, the FCC licenses television and radio frequencies, and thus broadcasters are obligated to obey decency rules. However, the FCC's power only extends to broadcast television, although the PTC and other organizations are seeking greater government control over cable networks.

Censorship of Art Exhibits

The U.S. government helps fund artists through the National Endowment for the Arts (NEA), which was established in 1965. The initial budget for the NEA was $2.5 million; in 2007 the organization received more than $124 million. While the budget has increased 50-fold, not all Americans support the NEA's mission. Many of the artists funded by the NEA have created works that are controversial and have sparked discussion over whether certain exhibits should be censored.

The NEA's funding of art that treats religion in a way that many people consider disrespectful has been the center of much of this debate. In 1988 Andres Serrano, as part of an exhibit funded by the NEA, submerged a crucifix in his urine, creating a

> " Many of the artists funded by the NEA have created works that are controversial and have sparked discussion over whether certain exhibits should be censored. "

work he entitled "Piss Christ." Eleven years later the Brooklyn Museum of Art displayed a painting by Chris Ofili called "Holy Virgin Mary," which consists of a black Virgin Mary decorated with pieces of elephant dung and sexually explicit pictures. New York was again the site of a contentious exhibit in March 2007. That time, controversy exploded over an exhibit at a Manhattan gallery titled "Chocolate Jesus." The sculpture by Cosimo Cavallaro was a nude, anatomically correct rendition of Jesus made out of chocolate. Catholic leaders, including Edward Cardinal Egan, head of the New York archdiocese, protested and sought a boycott of the hotel that housed the gallery. As a result, the sculpture was pulled.

Critics of these exhibits assert that the NEA and other public funding of art is wrong because it leads to the creation of what they consider blasphemous artwork. In fact, funding for the NEA fell by 40 percent during the 1990s. Cutting NEA funds can be considered a de facto form of government censorship because the endowment then has less money available to support artists. Some people seek more than to just reduce the NEA budget; conservative organizations such as Concerned Women for America have called for the NEA to be defunded entirely, charging that it serves as a government subsidy for offensive art and that private funding is sufficient to support art. Other people contend that public funding for the arts is acceptable but that such works should have broad public appeal.

Funding from other government sources has also been targeted. In response to the Ofili painting, then-mayor of New York City Rudolph W. Giuliani cut the city's funding of the Brooklyn museum from $24 million to $16 million. The museum sued Giuliani. A federal judge ruled in favor of the museum on November 1, 1999, stating that the mayor had violated the First Amendment and ordering him to restore full funding.

Supporters of public funding for the arts maintain that the amount of money spent on the NEA, compared with other pieces of the federal budget, is woefully meager and that to cut funding will further limit the ability of artists to create works. The NEA has already lost much of its power, art student Joan Bowlen argues. She declares, "Though the basic format of the NEA propagates . . . independent expression, the reality is that the federal government is still able to place crippling restraints on the NEA. . . . The agency is no longer able to fund independent artists due to Congressional concern over the types of works that result from individual grants."[33]

Censoring Cartoons

Political cartoons are intended to incite strong emotions, both from the people who agree with the views expressed by the artist and from those who oppose that opinion. However, some cartoons are so controversial that newspapers pull them. One comic strip that was frequently divisive during its run was *The Boondocks* by Aaron MacGruder. In the wake of the September 11, 2001, terrorist attacks, MacGruder drew a cartoon that implicitly compared President George W. Bush to Osama bin Laden, the man behind the attacks. Some newspapers dropped the strip in the wake of that and similar cartoons by MacGruder. Francis Beal, in a commentary for the Web site ZNet, asserts that the censorship of *The Boondocks* is disturbing because it suggests that people who satirize or ridicule the government will face serious consequences. *Doonesbury*, the long-running cartoon by Garry Trudeau, has been censored numerous times. For example, two newspapers pulled the strip after a November 2000 installment that accused presidential candidate George W. Bush of cocaine use. Other cartoonists have had strips pulled because of religious or homosexual content. Sometimes the cartoon is moved off the comics page and into the editorial section as a way to keep controversial themes away from younger readers.

Sometimes, newspaper editors argue, cartoons go too far and undermine the message they are trying to send. Jay Evensen of Salt Lake City's *Deseret Morning News* writes, "A certain amount of offense is tolerable, even instructive. After all, a lot of people find any opinion contrary to their own offensive. But somewhere along the offense spectrum lies a tipping point past which the average mind no longer stretches, it snaps."[34]

While many people view cartoon censorship as troubling, it pales in comparison to the deadly riots in Islamic nations that followed the publication of cartoons in a Danish newspaper that portrayed Muhammad, the founder of Islam, as a terrorist. These riots killed more than 100 people, while debate occurred over whether other newspapers should publish the cartoons in the interest of informing their readers.

> **Sometimes, newspaper editors argue, cartoons go too far and undermine the message they are trying to send.**

Banning Books

All types of art have been censored at one point, but no art form has a longer history of censorship than books. Whether they are burned or banned, books that delve into issues such as religion, sexuality, drugs, and race—among other topics—have been the target of censors for hundreds of years. In fact, some books have remained controversial long after their initial publication; *Huckleberry Finn* continues to cause debate over its use of a certain racial epithet. More recent titles that face censorship frequently include the Harry Potter series, because it purportedly encourages children to practice witchcraft, and the works of Judy Blume, because of how they deal with teenage sexuality. Parents and activists aim to have these and other books pulled from the shelves of schools and public libraries.

Banning books is a difficult task to achieve due to the Supreme Court's decision in *Board of Education, Island Trees v. Pico.* In that 1982 ruling the Court stated that school officials cannot remove books from school libraries because they disagree with the ideas in the books. The books considered in the *Pico* case included *Black Boy* by Richard Wright and *Slaughterhouse-Five* by Kurt Vonnegut. However, books have continued to be banned—or at the very least challenged—in the 25 years since the decision.

> **Artists need to be aware that their works will not always be well received by the government and their fellow citizens.**

In 2007 controversy erupted over an unlikely book—the Newberry Award winner, *The Higher Power of Lucky.* The award is the highest honor that a children's book can receive, making it highly likely that the book will be added to library shelves. In the case of *Higher Power*, however, many librarians were taken aback and refused to stock the book because the first page of the novel mentioned the word "scrotum," in reference to the title character overhearing a story about her neighbor's dog. One librarian, Dana Nilsson, explained to *Publisher's Weekly* that she did not add the book to the elementary school library where she works because "part of my job is to introduce students to quality, age-appropriate literature. . . . The inclusion of genitalia does not add to the story one bit and that is my objection."[35]

The response of Nilsson and other librarians has been decried as censorship by librarians and others who feel that by focusing on one word, people who oppose *Higher Power* are ignoring the overall merits of the book and the right of people to choose what books they would like to read. Others view the decision as hypocritical. David Hawpe of the *Louisville Courier-Journal* observes, "Here we are, one of the most oversexed societies on earth, awash in prurient popular culture, and we're arguing about whether kids ought to see the word 'scrotum.'"[36]

Art and Freedom

Art can be a powerful tool. It can bring beauty into lives while at the same time educating its patrons about important issues. However, artists need to be aware that their works will not always be well received by the government and their fellow citizens. Censorship is a reality that movie directors, authors, and other artists face regularly. The freedom to express oneself creatively is not limitless.

Primary Source Quotes*

Should the Media Be Censored?

66 **Decency groups feel they have power to decide what is aired on television, rather than the power to simply turn off the television.** 99

—PEN Center USA, "Censorship on Television: When Crying "Indecency" Goes Too Far," February 18, 2005.

PEN Center is an organization that works to defend the rights of writers around the world.

66 **It's time to acknowledge that the TV ratings adopted more than eight years ago have proved to be a shabby, irrelevant, hopelessly confusing failure.** 99

—Michael Medved, "The Mess of Mass Entertainment," April 18, 2005. www.townhall.com.

Medved is a film critic and radio talk-show host.

* Editor's Note: While the definition of a primary source can be narrowly or broadly defined, for the purposes of Compact Research, a primary source consists of: 1) results of original research presented by an organization or researcher; 2) eyewitness accounts of events, personal experience, or work experience; 3) first-person editorials offering pundits' opinions; 4) government officials presenting political plans and/or policies; 5) representatives of organizations presenting testimony or policy.

Primary Source Quotes

> ❝We conclude that a video broadcast image of Timberlake pulling off part of Jackson's bustier and exposing her bare breast, . . . is graphic and explicit.❞

—Statement of the Federal Communications Commission, February 21, 2006.

The FCC regulates television and radio communications.

> ❝Public funding for the arts does not allow the government to play the role of censor.❞

—Bill Kenworthy and Kyonzte Hughes, "Public Funding of Controversial Art," First Amendment Center, June 2006.

Kenworthy is a legal research assistant and Hughes a contributing writer for the First Amendment Center.

> ❝Before you get too carried away with condemning Muslims for being offended by the [Muhammad] cartoon, consider that even here in the spiritually illiterate part of the world, some things are considered out of bounds.❞

—Jay Evensen, "Some Cartoon Images Override Political Point," *Deseret Morning News*, February 12, 2006.

Evensen is the editor of the *Deseret Morning News* editorial page.

> ❝It wouldn't hurt for decency proponents to recognize that different people define 'values' differently [and] for media companies to take more seriously the genuine concerns of their customers.❞

—James Poniewozik, "The Decency Police," *Time*, March 20, 2005.

Poniewozik is *Time* magazine's media critic.

> 66 When a Web site is blocked on a library computer or a book is taken off the library shelves, it is easy to see how your freedom to access information is being compromised. 99

—American Civil Liberties Union, "Banned Books Week 2003," September 20, 2003.

The ACLU is an organization that aims to protect free speech, the right to privacy, and other civil liberties.

> 66 [The Harry Potter books have] evil themes, witchcraft, demonic activity, murder, evil blood sacrifice, spells and teaching children all of this. 99

—Laura Mallory, quoted in *Gwinnett Daily Post*, April 19, 2006.

Mallory is a Georgia woman who sought to have the Harry Potter series removed from local public school libraries.

> 66 The special characteristics of the school library make that environment especially appropriate for the recognition of the First Amendment rights of students. 99

—William Brennan, majority opinion in *Board of Education v. Pico*, June 25, 1982.

Brennan was a U.S. Supreme Court justice from 1956 until 1990.

Facts and Illustrations

Should the Media Be Censored?

- The largest fine in Federal Communications Commission history was **$1.2 million**, levied against the Fox network in 2004 for an episode of the show *Married by America*. The episode had included sexually explicit scenes of bachelor and bachelorette parties.

- A poll conducted by *Time* magazine found that **66 percent** of respondents felt that government officials overreacted to Janet Jackson's brief nudity during the 2004 Super Bowl half-time show.

- On average, PG-rated movies earn **five times** as much money as R-rated movies.

- Three of the most frequently **challenged authors** in 2005 were Judy Blume, Toni Morrison, and J.D. Salinger.

- The budget for the NEA in 2007 was **$124,412,000**.

- The Federal Communications Commission was established in 1934.

- Funding for the NEA fell by **40 percent** during the 1990s.

- The **Harry Potter** books were the most censored books from 1999 through 2002.

Comparing the Grosses of PG- and R-Rated Movies

Movie ratings are a way for parents to be informed of the content of films, but some people have argued that these ratings lead to self-censorship on the part of writers and directors. These tables show the highest-grossing PG- and R-rated movies in American movie history. The total gross of the top five films is $2,085,998,659, compared with $1,336,331,789 for the R-rated total. The results suggest that excluding potentially offensive material from movies makes them more lucrative.

PG-Rated Movies

Movie	Lifetime Gross	Year
1. *Star Wars*	$460,998,007	1977
2. *Shrek 2*	$441,226,247	2004
3. *E.T.: The Extra-Terrestrial*	$435,110,554	1982
4. *Star Wars: Episode I - The Phantom Menace*	$431,088,301	1999
5. *Harry Potter and the Sorcerer's Stone*	$317,575,550	2001

R-Rated Movies

Movie	Lifetime Gross	Year
1. *The Passion of the Christ*	$370,782,930	2004
2. *The Matrix Reloaded*	$281,576,461	2003
3. *Beverly Hills Cop*	$234,760,478	1984
4. *The Exorcist*	$232,671,011	1973
5. *Saving Private Ryan*	$216,540,909	1998

Source: Boxofficemojo.com, "All-Time Box Office: Domestic Grosses by MPAA Rating," 2007.

Americans Do Not Support Banning Adult Content on Television

In a 2005 study conducted by the research company SBRI, the majority of adults polled agreed that television contains too much violence, foul language, and sexual content. However, by a significant percentage they do not believe that the government should ban such material. This poll suggests that television censorship is largely an unpopular idea.

Too Much on TV?	Too Much	Yes, Ban
Violence	66%	36%
"Reality" TV	65%	18%
Cursing	58%	41%
Televised Plastic Surgery	51%	21%
Sexual Content/Nudity	50%	41%
Homosexuality	50%	35%
Drug/Alcohol Abuse	46%	33%

Source: Schulman, Ronca, and Bucuvala, Inc., SRBI Public Affairs Poll, "Americans: Too Much Sex and Violence on TV—but Government Over-Reacted to Janet Jackson 'Malfunction,'" March 18, 2005.

- **143** movies have received NC-17 ratings since that designation was established in 1990. Many of those movies were then edited so that they could be released with R ratings.

- The first library to ban *Huckleberry Finn* was the public library in Concord, Massachusetts, which did so in **1885**, the year the book was published.

Americans Feel Parents Should Regulate Television Content Viewed by Children

In your view, who should be primarily responsible for keeping inappropriate material on television away from children: Parents, Government officials or Broadcasters?

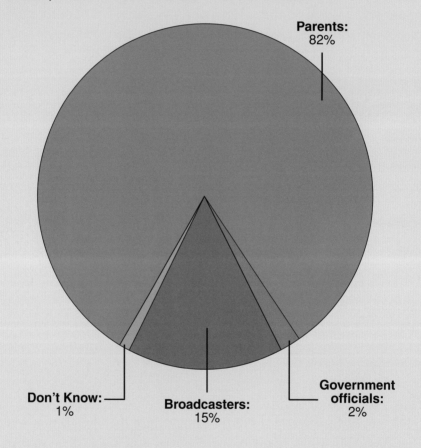

Parents:
82%

Don't Know:
1%

Broadcasters:
15%

Government officials:
2%

By an overwhelming margin, American adults polled by the First Amendment Center believe that parents, rather than the government or television networks, are the people who should keep inappropriate material out of the view of children.

Source: First Amendment Center, *2006 State of the First Amendment Survey*, November 11, 2006.

NEA Appropriations, 1966 to 2004

This chart shows that the amount of money given to the National Endowment for the Arts has increased significantly since 1966. However, it also indicates that current funding has dropped far below its peak in the early 1990s, athough the funding has increased by more than 20 percent since being reduced by more than $60 million between 1995 and 1996. Government reduction in art funding is considered a form of censorship if it occurs because politicians do not want to give money to subsidize art that they consider offensive.

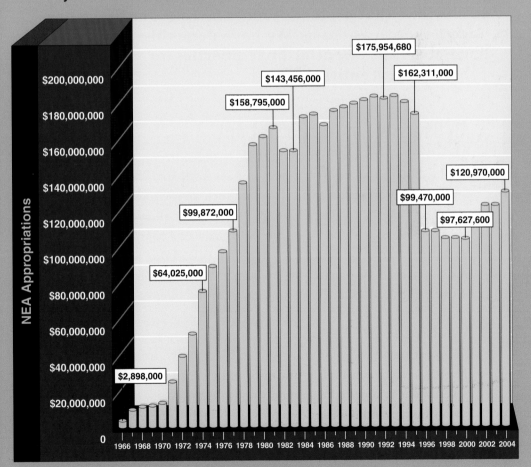

Source: Americans for the Arts Action Fund, Congressional Arts Report Card, October 2004.

Are the Free Speech Limits in the Patriot Act Justified?

> **The laws that protect us must be relevant to the dangers that threaten us. We have done this without sacrificing the essential civil liberties to which every American is entitled.**

—Chuck Hagel, press release on the Patriot Act.

An Overview of the Patriot Act

American foreign and domestic policy changed irrevocably on September 11, 2001. The terrorist attacks in New York and Washington, D.C. that killed 3,000 people led to fear that such an event could repeat itself and debate over how America could best protect itself in the future. Congress responded to the debate with the passage of a controversial bill that became law on October 26, 2001. The full title of this act is the Uniting and Strengthening America by Providing Appropriate Tools Required to Intercept and Obstruct Terrorism Act, but it is better known as the USA Patriot Act, or simply the Patriot Act.

The purpose of the Patriot Act is to strengthen the ability of the federal government to stop terrorists from successfully carrying out attacks. The act aims to accomplish this mission by expanding the ability of the government to order wiretaps and warrantless searches, read e-mails, and review library and bookstore records. Although Congress passed the Patriot Act by overwhelming votes—337 to 79 in the House of Representatives and 98 to 1 in the Senate (Wisconsin senator Russ Feingold was the sole no vote in his chamber)—the adoption of the act has not been lauded universally. Critics of the act on both ends of the political spectrum contend that in its desire to strengthen national security, the U.S. government has destroyed free speech and other civil liberties.

The different elements of the Patriot Act have led to debate over whether civil liberties or national security should take precedence in America.

A major concern cited by civil liberties organizations is that Congress passed the Patriot Act with little understanding of what the legislation contained. The American Civil Liberties Union notes that members of Congress had as little as one hour to read the 342-page bill. Consequently, the federal government was granted powers that might have been pared down or eliminated had more debate been possible. Only one month transpired between the Bush administration's submitting antiterrorism legislation to Congress and the passage of the Patriot Act.

However, criticism of the Patriot Act has not been limited to free-speech and civil-liberties organizations. According to Nancy Kranich, a senior research fellow for the Free Expression Policy Project, three states and 149 cities, towns, and counties passed resolutions to protect the civil liberties of their citizens. These Civil Liberties Safe Zone resolutions call for their senators and representatives to work toward repealing the Patriot Act and urge law enforcement to avoid activities that threaten civil liberties.

> " The different elements of the Patriot Act have led to debate over whether civil liberties or national security should take precedence in America. "

Supporters of the Patriot Act respond to these concerns by noting that there has not been another attack on U.S. soil since September 11, an indication that the legislation has been effective in protecting American citizens. Former U.S. attorney general John Ashcroft has stated, "We are arresting and detaining potential terrorist threats . . . [and] dismantling the terrorist financial network."[37] In testimony before the U.S. House of Representatives Permanent Committee on Intelligence, Paul Rosenzweig, a senior legal research fellow at the Heritage Foundation, defended the act. According to Rosenzweig, "Whatever one may think of the steps that the domestic law enforcement and intelligence agencies are taking to combat terror during today's crisis, I think it is undeniable that the actions today are more moderate and restrained than those of the past."[38]

Are Wiretaps Justified?

Section 216 of the Patriot Act gives the National Security Agency the power to monitor phone calls and e-mails without first receiving a warrant. In particular, the section allows for roving wiretaps, or taps on every phone and computer that might be used by the person under surveillance. The intent is for the government to be able to listen in on terrorist plots, but the concern is that the government is spying on people whose conversations pose no threat.

U.S. attorney general Alberto Gonzales defended the use of wiretaps in an interview with CNN. According to Gonzales, "A very important aspect of engaging in war against the enemy is to engage in signal intelligence. Signal intelligence means that we have to know what our enemy is doing. We can't go into a war blindly. We've engaged in signal intelligence beginning with the Civil War and through all the conflicts since then."[39] Terrorism expert Harvey Kushner contends that roving wiretaps are important in the fight against terrorism because they allow for the tracking of calls made on satellite phones.

> Critics of wiretaps charge that the policy violates both a person's right to free speech and right to privacy.

Wiretaps go too far, in others' opinions. They believe that the government does not have the right to listen to the private conversations of its citizens, particularly when the people being surveilled have no idea that they are the targets of an investigation. Critics of wiretaps charge that the policy violates both a person's right to free speech and right to privacy. Another issue is that sometimes the wrong phone is tapped and authorities listen in on the conversations of people who are not even suspected of wrongdoing.

The response by the judicial system has been mixed. In August 2006 U.S. district judge Anna Diggs Taylor found the White House's use of wiretaps an unconstitutional infringement on free speech. Taylor also stated that the wiretapping program violated the Foreign Intelligence

Surveillance Act, which requires the executive branch to receive a warrant before eavesdropping on phone calls. The government requested a stay during the appeals process. Meanwhile, in February 2007 the California Supreme Court upheld the use of wiretaps, stating that they are necessary if normal investigation procedures are unlikely to succeed.

Government Review of Library and Bookstore Records

One of the most controversial elements of the Patriot Act is Section 215, which allows law enforcement to obtain library and bookstore records "to protect against international terrorism or clandestine intelligence activities." Opposition to Section 215 is based on the idea that it allows the FBI to find out the reading habits of innocent Americans and places librarians and bookstore owners in the uncomfortable position of revealing private information about their patrons and customers. A further concern is that people who read books about terrorism because they are interested in expanding their knowledge on the subject might be mistaken for people who sympathize with terrorist activity.

> " Opposition to Section 215 is based on the idea that it allows the FBI to find out the reading habits of innocent Americans. "

The American Library Association (ALA) is one of the most vocal critics of Section 215. It urges librarians to defend the privacy of its patrons and to become educated in the process of complying with the Patriot Act. The ALA also encourages librarians "to adopt and implement patron privacy and record retention policies that affirm that 'the collection of personally identifiable information should only be a matter of routine or policy when necessary for the fulfillment of the mission of the library.'"[40] In the view of the ALA, Section 215 and other parts of the Patriot Act threaten the Constitution and suppress the free exchange of knowledge.

Former attorney general John Ashcroft contends that such fears are overblown. In a speech in September 2003, Ashcroft declared, "The law enforcement community has no interest in your reading habits. Tracking reading habits would betray our high regard for the First Amendment. . . . With only 11,000 FBI agents in the entire country, it is simply ridiculous to think we could or would track what citizens are reading."[41] His views are supported by Rachel Donadio, who in an article for the *New York Times* writes that despite the uproar, few librarians and booksellers can point out situations where their privacy or that of their patrons has been invaded. In fact, the Department of Justice has used the power afforded it by Section 215 only three dozen times.

Are Specific Groups Targeted?

The weeks immediately following the September 11 attacks were particularly difficult for Muslim Americans, who were targets of hate crimes by people who associated all Muslims with terrorism. Concerns have been raised that the Patriot Act further stigmatizes this group of Americans.

John Tirnan, writing for the *Christian Science Monitor*, asserts that Muslim Americans have been the target of antiterrorism legislation, in particular, surveillance. In addition, he observes, "Speech is constrained—self-censored, but also restricted by Washington's actions."[42] However, Tirnan writes, the Patriot Act has turned up little evidence of domestic terrorist cells. David Cole, an attorney at the Center for Constitutional Rights, asserts in an interview with the PBS program *Frontline* that the act criminalizes foreign nationals based entirely on their speech.

> " **Writers are another group at risk under the Patriot Act.** "

Writers are another group at risk under the Patriot Act. Mystery author Sara Paretsky, writing for the magazine the *New Statesman*, recalled that several years earlier, one of her books was very briefly part of a murder investigation. With the Patriot Act in existence, Paretsky now fears that she could face imprisonment if her novels were believed by law enforcement to have connections to terrorist-related crimes. Such concerns can make Paretsky and other authors fearful about what they should and should not write. Consequently, writes syndicated columnist and journalism professor Walt Brasch, "If the Act is not modified . . . writers may not create the works that a free nation should read."[43]

Congressional Response to the Patriot Act

Congress reauthorized the Patriot Act in March 2006, but not before making some changes to the law. Several provisions are set to expire in

March 2010, including Section 215, although other provisions became permanent. A newer version of the act, Patriot Act II, which would make it easier for federal authorities to get information from Internet service providers, has not passed; however, some of its proposed statutes have been included in other legislation.

Opposition to the Patriot Act is much stronger at present than in 2001. The ACLU points out that in 2005, 11 senators opposed reauthorization of the act, while both parties in the House of Representatives sought to add checks and balances to the legislation. However, even with the growing discontent over the Patriot Act, civil liberties fears remain. In the view of the ACLU the amended Patriot Act still fails to protect privacy rights.

Has the Patriot Act Been Effective?

Despite the claims made by the Bush administration, not everyone believes that the Patriot Act has been the appropriate response to terrorism. Tom Maertens, a former staff member of the White House National Security Council, suggests that the government should consider another approach: "We can expect terrorist attempts in the future, but mass roundups under the USA Patriot Act are not the way to prevent another 9/11; international and interagency sharing of data and better coordination are."[44]

> Despite the claims made by the Bush administration, not everyone believes that the Patriot Act has been the appropriate response to terrorism.

Syndicated columnist Michelle Malkin points to the many successes of the Patriot Act, including the convictions or guilty pleas of more than 100 people for terrorist-related crimes, as proof that the act is necessary and successful. She also defends the act against charges that it infringes on civil liberties, contending that such claims are histrionic and that its critics ignore the fact that the Supreme Court has upheld every major initiative of the legislation.

No terrorist attacks have occurred on U.S. soil since September 11, 2001, and the subsequent passage of the Patriot Act, which may suggest that the act is serving its purpose and that this success outweighs any concerns about censorship and free speech. A better understanding of the impact of the Patriot Act may not occur until some of its provisions have expired, in particular Section 215, and as the court system continues to consider the issue of wiretaps. Until that time it may be difficult to determine whether a successful balance has been maintained between free speech and national security.

Primary Source Quotes*

Are the Free Speech Limits in the Patriot Act Justified?

66 With only 11,000 FBI agents in the entire country, it is simply ridiculous to think we could or would track what citizens are reading. 99

—John Ashcroft, "The Proven Tactics in the Fight Against Crime," address before the National Restaurant Association, Washington, D.C., September 15, 2003.

Ashcroft is a former U.S attorney general.

....

66 The marketing department of any given publishing house probably has far more power over free expression in America than any government office. 99

—Rachel Donadio, "Is There Censorship?" *New York Times*, December 19, 2004.

Donadio is the editor of the *New York Times Book Review*.

....

Bracketed quotes indicate conflicting positions.

* Editor's Note: While the definition of a primary source can be narrowly or broadly defined, for the purposes of Compact Research, a primary source consists of: 1) results of original research presented by an organization or researcher; 2) eyewitness accounts of events, personal experience, or work experience; 3) first-person editorials offering pundits' opinions; 4) government officials presenting political plans and/or policies; 5) representatives of organizations presenting testimony or policy.

❝The American Library Association urges librarians everywhere to defend and support user privacy and free and open access to knowledge and information.❞

—American Library Association, "Resolution on the USA Patriot Act and Related Measures That Infringe on the Rights of Library Users," January 29, 2003.

The ALA helps develop and improve library services.

❝The Director of the Federal Bureau of Investigation or a designee of the Director . . . may make an application for an order requiring the production of any tangible things (including books, records, papers, documents, and other items) for an investigation to protect against international terrorism.❞

—USA Patriot Act, Section 215, October 24, 2001.

The Patriot Act became law on December 26, 2001.

❝No First Amendment liberties have been curtailed, no dissent or criticism suppressed [by the Patriot Act.]❞

—Paul Rosenzweig, "The Ashcroft Legacy: Liberty and Security," *WebMemo #607*, Heritage Foundation, November 10, 2004.

Rosenzweig is a lawyer and former Justice Department trial attorney.

❝The PATRIOT Act and related measures chill civil liberties, particularly free expression.❞

—Nancy Kranich, "The Impact of the USA PATRIOT Act: An Update," Free Expression Policy Project, August 27, 2003.

Kranich is a senior research fellow at the Free Expression Policy Project.

66 **Freedom of speech, even dissent, is not just at the core of our freedom, it is an essential component of security.** 99

—Paul K. McMasters, "Spying as a Form of Censorship," First Amendment Center, August 27, 2006.

McMasters is the ombudsman of the First Amendment Center.

66 **When assessing civil liberty questions, it is important not to lose sight of the underlying purpose of government: personal and national security.** 99

—The Heritage Foundation, *Heritage Special Report: The Patriot Act Reader*, September 20, 2004.

The Heritage Foundation is a think tank that supports limited government.

66 **If there is no clear end to the war, it will be difficult to end the threat to civil liberties.** 99

—George H. Pike, "USA Patriot Act: What's Next?" *Information Today*, April 2006.

Pike is an assistant professor of law at the University of Pittsburgh School of Law.

66 **[The wiretapping] program is conscious of people's civil liberties, as am I.** 99

—George W. Bush, quoted on CNN, January 1, 2006.

Bush is the 43rd president of the United States.

66 **The [wiretapping program] violates . . . the First and Fourth Amendments of the United States Constitution.** 99

—Anna Diggs Taylor, decision in *ACLU et al. v. National Security Agency*, August 17, 2006.

Taylor is a U.S. district court judge.

Are the Free Speech Limits in the Patriot Act Justified?

- More than **400 communities** have passed resolutions seeking reforms of the Patriot Act.

- During 2005, **1,773 wiretaps** were completed.

- In August 2002, **22 percent** of people polled by Gallup felt that the Patriot Act went too far. By April 2005 that number had risen to **45 percent.**

- Only one senator, Russ Feingold of Wisconsin, **voted against** the Patriot Act.

- In response to a survey in February 2002, **85 percent** of librarians stated that police or FBI agents had requested information about their patrons.

- The Patriot Act was renewed in March 2006 by a vote of **89 to 11** in the Senate and 280 to 138 in the House of Representatives.

- U.S. courts have struck down **two Patriot Act** provisions that deal with free speech. One required banks, Internet service providers, and others to reveal information about customers. The other involved a ban on assisting terrorist organizations.

- The FBI did not use **Section 215** between 2002 and 2005; how often it was used in 2006 was not known as of March 2007.

Civil Liberties Should Not Be Sacrificed in Fight Against Terrorism

"In order to curb terrorism in this country, do you think it will be necessary for the average person to give up some civil liberties, or not?"

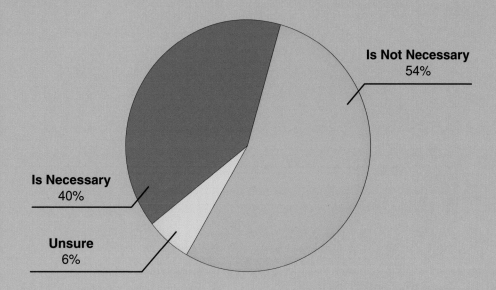

Is Not Necessary
54%

Is Necessary
40%

Unsure
6%

In a poll conducted by the Pew Research Center, more than half of the respondents believed that American citizens should not give up civil liberties in the fight against terrorism. These results indicate that the average person believes that security and liberty do not need to be opposing propositions.

Source: Pew Research Center for the People & the Press survey, December 12, 2006–January 9, 2007.

Views on Wiretapping

As you may know, the Bush administration has been wiretapping telephone conversations between U.S. citizens living in the United States and suspected terrorists living in other countries without getting a court order allowing it to do so. Do you think the Bush administration was right or wrong in wiretapping these conversations without obtaining a court order?

September 15–17, 2006

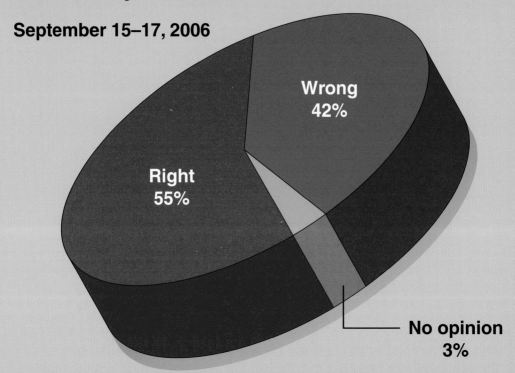

Wrong
42%

Right
55%

No opinion
3%

A poll conducted by Gallup shows that, on average, slightly over half of Americans believe that the Bush administration was right to wiretap conversations involving suspected terrorists without receiving a court order. Although wiretapping is a antiterrorist tactic that has been widely criticized by free-speech advocates, the results of this poll suggest that it is not a concern for a large percentage of Americans.

Source: Gallup's Pulse of Democracy, "The Patriot Act and Civil Liberties," 2006.

Increases in Wiretapping

This graph shows that the number of wiretaps authorized by state and federal courts increased sharply in the wake of the September 11 terrorist attacks and the Patriot Act. In 2005, 1,773 wiretaps were authorized.

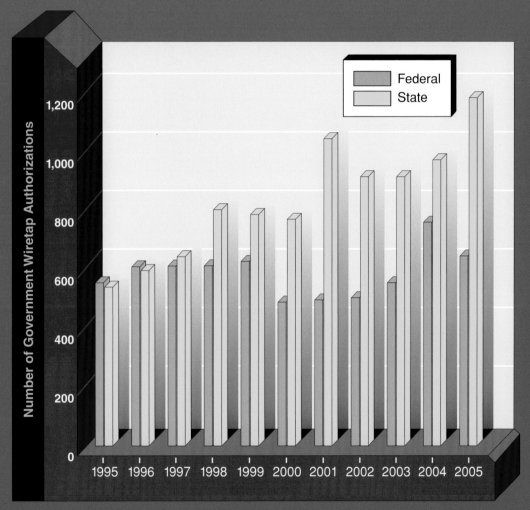

Source: *Report of the Director of the Administrative Offcie of the United States Courts on Applications for Orders Authorizing or Approving the Interception of Wire, Oral, or Electronic Communications*, April 2006.

Key People and Advocacy Groups

American Civil Liberties Union: Founded in 1920, the ACLU is a nonprofit organization known for its support of free speech and the First Amendment.

Brent Bozell: Bozell is the founder of the Parents Television Council, an organization that targets indecency on television.

Viet Dinh: Dinh is a former assistant attorney general of the United States. He authored the USA Patriot Act.

Oliver Wendell Holmes: Holmes was a Supreme Court justice who penned the decision in *Schenck v. United States* (1919), in which he stated that censorship is permissible if the government can prove that a person's words or actions pose a real and imminent threat.

James Madison and George Mason: Madison and Mason were Virginia politicians who helped write the Bill of Rights.

John Stuart Mill: Mill was a nineteenth-century English philosopher who wrote frequently about the importance of free speech, including in his book *On Liberty.*

National Coalition Against Censorship: The coalition, founded in 1974, is a collection of 50 nonprofit organizations that believe free expression must be defended. It seeks to educate people about threats to free expression.

Jack Valenti: Valenti was the president of the Motion Picture Association of America from 1996 until 2004. In 1968 he abolished the Hays Code and replaced it with the movie ratings system.

John Peter Zenger: Zenger was a New York journalist and publisher who was arrested and imprisoned on charges of libel in 1734, the result of articles published in his newspaper that were critical of the colony's governor. Zenger was acquitted, a decision that helped establish freedom of the press in the United States.

Chronology

1735
Publisher John Peter Zenger is acquitted of libel after publishing criticism of the Royal Governor of New York.

1776
George Mason advocates for freedom of the press in the Virginia Declaration of Rights.

1873
The Comstock Law, which makes it illegal for people to send obscene materials through the mail, is passed by Congress.

1918
Congress passes the Sedition Act, a law that forbids printed and spoken criticism of the American flag, the Constitution, and the federal government.

1921
Congress repeals the Sedition Act.

1930
The Hays Code, which places restrictions on the content of movies, is created.

1968
The Motion Picture Association of Americ (MPAA) establishes a movie ratings system.

1942
In its ruling in *Chaplinsky v. New Hampshire*, the Supreme Court states that "fighting words"—words that immediately lead to a breach of peace—are not protected free speech.

A.D.

1700   1750   1800   1900   1910   1920   1930   1940   1950   1960

1791
The Bill of Rights is ratified.

1798
The Alien and Sedition Acts are passed. These acts make it a crime to publish "any false, scandalous and malicious writing" against the government.

1769
British thinker William Blackstone argues for freedom of the press in *Commentaries on the Laws of England*.

1919
The Supreme Court rules in *Schenck v. U.S.* that not all speech is protected by the First Amendment—in particular, speech that creates "a clear and present danger."

1920
The American Civil Liberties Union (ACLU) is founded.

1941
Congress passes the First War Powers Act, which gives President Franklin D. Roosevelt the authority to censor mail and other communications between the United States and foreign nations. Roosevelt also creates the Office of Censorship, whose employees examine private and public communications.

1957
In its decision in *Roth v. United States*, the Supreme Court declares that obscenity is not constitutionally protected and that communities must determine what materials they consider obscene.

1952
The Supreme Court rules in *Burstyn v. Wilson* that movies are protected under the First Amendment.

Chronology

84

1982
In *Board v. Pico*, the U.S. Supreme Court rules that school officials cannot remove books from school libraries because they disagree with the ideas in the books; the Court rules in *New York v. Ferber* that child pornography is not a protected form of free speech.

2000
Congress enacts the Children's Internet Protection Act. The law requires any library or school that receives funding from the "E-rate" program to meet certain requirements—in particular, installing Internet filters.

1969
The Supreme Court rules in *Tinker v. Des Moines Independent School District* that school officials cannot censor the free expression of students unless such expression could substantially disrupt school activities.

1989
The U.S. Supreme Court rules in *Texas v. Johnson* that burning the American flag is protected free speech.

1998
Congress passes the Child Online Protection Act, which makes the transmission of commercial material "harmful to minors" on the Internet a federal crime. The law will be repeatedly ruled unconstitutional.

1970 1975 1980 1985 1990 1995 2000

1973
In its decision in *Miller v. California*, the U.S. Supreme Court rules that obscene speech is not protected under the First Amendment and establishes three criteria that have to be met for material to be considered obscene.

1992
The U.S. Supreme Court invalidates a hate speech ordinance in its *R.A.V. v. City of St. Paul* decision, explaining that the ordinance violates the First Amendment.

2001
Congress passes the Patriot Act, legislation intended to prevent terrorism that gives the federal government more power to read e-mails and wiretap phone conversations.

1988
In its decision in *Hazelwood School District v. Kuhlmeier*, the U.S. Supreme Court rules that school officials may censor school-sponsored student publications.

1996
Congress passes the Communications Decency Act. The law prohibits "indecent" materials from being posted on public forums on the Internet, such as chat rooms and newsgroups.

2003
The U.S. Supreme Court upholds CIPA (Children's Internet Protection Act) in its decision in *United States v. American Library Association*.

1997
In its decision in *Reno v. ACLU*, the U.S. Supreme Court rules that the Communications Decency Act is unconstitutional because it interferes with the free speech rights of adults.

Related Organizations

American Civil Liberties Union (ACLU)
125 Broad St., 18th Fl.
New York, NY 10004
phone: (212) 549-2500 • fax: (212) 549-2646
e-mail: aclu@aclu.org • Web site: www.aclu.org

The ACLU is a national organization that defends Americans' civil rights guaranteed in the U.S. Constitution. It adamantly opposes regulation of all forms of speech, including pornography and hate speech. The ACLU offers numerous reports, fact sheets, and policy statements on a wide variety of issues. Publications include "Freedom of Expression," "Hate Speech on Campus," and "Free Speech Under Fire."

American Library Association (ALA)
50 E. Huron St.
Chicago, IL 60611
phone: (800) 545-2433 • fax: (312) 440-9374
e-mail: ala@ala.org • Web site: www.ala.org

The ALA is the nation's primary professional organization for librarians. Through its Office for Intellectual Freedom, the ALA supports free access to libraries and library materials. The OIF also monitors and opposes efforts to ban books. The ALA's sister organization, the Freedom to Read Foundation, provides legal defense for libraries. Publications include *American Libraries*, *Newsletter on Intellectual Freedom*, articles, fact sheets, and policy statements.

Concerned Women for America (CWA)
1015 15th St. NW, Suite 1100
Washington, DC 20005
phone: (202) 488-7000 • fax: (202) 488-0806
Web site: www.cwfa.org

CWA is a membership organization that promotes conservative values and is concerned with creating an environment that is conducive to building strong families and raising healthy children. CWA publishes the monthly *Family Voice*, which argues against all forms of pornography.

Electronic Frontier Foundation (EFF)
454 Shotwell St.
San Francisco CA 94110-1914
phone: (415) 436-9333 • fax: (415) 436-9993
e-mail: information@eff.org • Web site: www.eff.org

EFF is a nonprofit, nonpartisan organization that works to protect privacy and freedom of expression in the arena of computers and the Internet. Its missions include supporting litigation that protects First Amendment rights. EFF's Web site publishes an electronic bulletin, *Effector*, and the guidebook *Protecting Yourself Online: The Definitive Resource on Safety, Freedom & Privacy in Cyberspace.*

Family Research Council (FRC)
801 G St. NW
Washington, DC 20001
phone: (202) 393-2100 • fax: (202) 393-2134
e-mail: corrdept@frc.org • Web site: www.frc.org

The Family Research Council is an organization that believes pornography degrades women and children and seeks to strengthen current obscenity laws. It publishes brochures, booklets, and fact sheets, including "Dealing with Pornography."

Freedom Forum
1101 Wilson Blvd.
Arlington, VA 22209
phone: (703) 528-0800 • fax: (703) 284-3770
e-mail: news@freedomforum.org • Web site: www.freedomforum.org

The Freedom Forum is an international organization that works to protect freedom of the press and free speech. It monitors developments in media and First Amendment issues on its Web site. Publications available from Freedom Forum include "Different Wars, Similar Fears," "State of the First Amendment 2005," and "Internet Filters and Public Libraries."

International Freedom of Expression Exchange (IFEX)

555 Richmond St. W., PO Box #407
Toronto, ON, Canada M5V 3B1
phone: (416) 515-9622 • fax: (416) 515-7879
e-mail: ifex@ifex.org • Web site: www.ifex.org

IFEX consists of more than 40 organizations that support the freedom of expression. Its work is coordinated by the Toronto-based Clearing House. Through the Action Alert Network, organizations report abuses of free expression to the Clearing House, which distributes that information throughout the world. Publications include the weekly *Communiqué*, which reports on developments and issues relating to free expression.

Morality in Media (MIM)

475 Riverside Dr., Suite 239
New York, NY 10115
phone: (212) 870-3222 • fax: (212) 870-2765
e-mail: mim@moralityinmedia.org
Web site: www.moralityinmedia.org

Morality in Media is an interfaith organization that fights obscenity and opposes indecency in the mainstream media. It believes pornography harms society and maintains the National Obscenity Law Center, a clearinghouse of legal materials on obscenity law. MIM publishes a quarterly newsletter and the law center publishes a bimonthly bulletin.

National Coalition Against Censorship (NCAC)

275 Seventh Ave., #1504
New York, NY 10001
phone: (212) 807-6222 • fax: (212) 807-6245
e-mail: ncac@ncac.org • Web site: www.ncac.org

The coalition represents more than 40 national organizations that work to prevent suppression of free speech and the press. NCAC educates the public about the dangers of censorship and provides information on issues such as Internet filters and political dissent. The coalition publishes the quarterly newsletter *Censorship News*.

National Coalition for the Protection of Children & Families

800 Compton Rd., Suite 9224
Cincinnati, OH 45231-9964
phone: (513) 521-6227 • fax: (513) 521-6337
Web site: www.nationalcoalition.org

The coalition is an organization of business, religious, and civic leaders who work to eliminate pornography. It encourages citizens to support the enforcement of obscenity laws and to close down neighborhood pornography outlets. Brochures on the effects of pornography are available for sale on its Web site.

People for the American Way (PFAW)

2000 M St. NW, Suite 400
Washington, DC 20036
phone: (202) 467-4999 or (800) 326-PFAW
e-mail: pfaw@pfaw.org • Web site: www.pfaw.org

PFAW works to promote citizen participation in democracy and to safeguard the principles of the U.S. Constitution, including the right to free speech. It publishes a variety of fact sheets, articles, and position statements on its Web site.

For Further Research

Books

George Anastaplo, *Reflections on Freedom of Speech and the First Amendment.* Lexington: University Press of Kentucky, 2007.

Robert Atkins and Svetlana Mintcheva, eds., *Censoring Culture: Contemporary Threats to Free Expression.* New York: New Press, 2006.

Joan Axelrod-Contrada, *Reno v. ACLU: Internet Censorship.* Tarrytown, NY: Marshall Cavendish Benchmark, 2007.

Randall P. Bezanson, *How Free Can the Press Be?* Urbana: University of Illinois Press, 2003.

David Cole, *Terrorism and the Constitution: Sacrificing Civil Liberties in the Name of National Security.* New York: New Press, 2006.

Anthony Cortese, *Opposing Hate Speech.* Westport, CT: Praeger, 2006.

David Dadge, ed., *Silenced: International Journalists Expose Media Censorship.* Amherst, NY: Prometheus, 2005.

Donald Alexander Downs, *Restoring Free Speech and Liberty on Campus.* Oakland, CA: Independent Institute, 2005.

Amitai Etzioni, *How Patriotic Is the Patriot Act? Freedom Versus Security in the Age of Terrorism.* New York: Routledge, 2004.

Ian C. Friedman, *Freedom of Speech and the Press.* New York: Facts On File, 2005.

Katharine Gelber, *Speaking Back: The Free Speech Versus Hate Speech Debate.* Philadelphia: J. Benjamins, 2002.

Ted Gottfried, *Censorship.* New York: Marshall Cavendish Benchmark, 2006.

Jon B. Gould, *Speak No Evil: The Triumph of Hate Speech Regulation.* Chicago: University of Chicago Press, 2005.

John B. Harer and Jeanne Harrell, *People for and Against Restricted or Unrestricted Expression.* Westport, CT: Greenwood, 2002.

Charles Haynes et al., *The First Amendment in Schools.* Alexandria, VA: Association for Supervision and Curriculum Development, 2003.

John H. Houchin, *Censorship of the American Theatre in the Twentieth Century.* Cambridge: Cambridge University Press, 2003.

Russ Kick, ed., *Abuse Your Illusions: The Disinformation Guide to Media Mirages and Establishment Lies.* New York: Disinformation, 2003.

Rebecca Knuth, *Libricide: The Regime-Sponsored Destruction of Books and Libraries in the Twentieth Century.* Westport, CT: Praeger, 2003.

Judith Levine, *Harmful to Minors: The Perils of Protecting Children from Sex.* Minneapolis: University of Minnesota Press, 2002.

Nan Levinson, *Outspoken: Free Speech Stories.* Berkeley and Los Angeles: University of California Press, 2003.

Office of Intellectual Freedom for the American, *Intellectual Freedom Manual.* Chicago: American Library Association, 2002.

Diane Ravitch, *The Language Police: How Pressure Groups Restrict What Students Learn.* New York: Knopf, 2003.

David L. Robb, *Operation Hollywood: How the Pentagon Shapes and Censors the Movies.* Amherst, NY: Prometheus, 2004.

Kevin W. Saunders, *Saving Our Children from the First Amendment.* New York: New York University Press, 2003.

Geoffrey R. Stone, *Perilous Times: Free Speech in Wartime from the Sedition Act of 1798 to the War on Terrorism.* New York: Norton, 2005.

Keith Werhan, *Freedom of Speech: A Reference Guide to the United States Constitution.* Westport, CT: Praeger, 2004.

Periodicals

Mary Ann Bell, "The Elephant in the Room," *School Library Journal,* January 2007.

Julie Bosman, "With One Word, Children's Book Sets Off Uproar," *New York Times,* February 18, 2007.

Economist, "Free Speech Under Threat," October 21, 2006.

Laura Flanders, "Librarians Under Siege," *Nation*, August 5, 2002.

Ronald Lee Fleming and Melissa Tapper Goldman, "Public Art for the Public," *Public Interest*, Spring 2005.

Nick Gillespie, "Express Yourself," *Reason*, May 2004.

Rachel Gillett, "Shrinking Free Speech Zones," *Humanist*, March/April 2005.

Jonah Goldberg, "Free Speech Rots from the Inside Out," *American Enterprise*, January /February 2003.

Robert Hughes, "Free Libraries, Free Society," *American Libraries*, August 2002.

Charles L. Klotzer, "Censorship: A Two-Front War," *St. Louis Journalism Review*, April 2003.

William Kristol, "Oh, the Anguish! The Cartoon Jihad Is Phony," *Weekly Standard*, February 20, 2006.

John Leo, "Campus Censors in Retreat," *U.S. News & World Report*, February 16, 2004.

Anthony Lewis, "Law and Journalism in Times of Crisis," *Advocate*, November 2003.

Stephen Lubet, "Toward Purposeful Dissent," *American Legion Magazine*, June 2004.

Douglas MacMillan, "Nations That Censor the Net," *Business Week Online*, November 10, 2006.

Gary Pavela, "Only Speech Codes Should Be Censored," *Chronicle of Higher Education*, December 1, 2006.

Agnes Poirier, "When Did You Forget to Defend Freedom?" *New Statesman*, February 19, 2007.

Joe Saltzman, "It Can't Happen Here," *USA Today* magazine, September 2003.

Alisa Solomon, "The Big Chill," *Nation*, June 2, 2003.

Patrick Tucker, "Speech Codes and the Future of Education," *Futurist*, March/April 2006.

USA Today, "Schools Fail Free Speech 101," February 12, 2007.

Barbara Dafoe Whitehead, "Online Porn: How Do We Keep It from Our Kids?" *Commonweal*, October 21, 2005.

Internet Sources

American Civil Liberties Union, *Freedom Under Fire: Dissent in Post-9/11 America*, May 2003. www.aclu.org.

Foundation for Individual Rights in Education, *Spotlight on Speech Codes 2006: The State of Free Speech on Our Nation's Campuses*, December 6, 2006. www.thefire.org.

Paul Rosenzweig, Alane Kochems, and James Jay Carafano, eds., *Heritage Special Report: The Patriot Act Reader*, September 20, 2004. www.heritage.org.

David L. Sobel, "Internet Filters and Public Libraries," First Amendment Center, October 2003. www.firstamendmentcenter.org.

Geoffrey R. Stone, interviewed by Ronald K.L. Collins, "Different War, Similar Fears: An Interview About Government Restrictions on Free Speech in Wartime," *First Amendment Center First Reports*, November 2004. www.firstamendmentcenter.org.

Patrick A. Trueman, *Dealing with Pornography: A Practical Guide for Protecting Your Family and Your Community.* Washington, DC: Family Research Council, 2005. www.frc.org.

Source Notes

Overview

1. Nadine Strossen, "Hate Speech: What Price Tolerance?" remarks at the Arlin M. Adams Center for Law and Society, Susquehanna University, March 13, 2003. http://susqu.edu.
2. Jonah Goldberg, "Free Speech Rots from the Inside Out," *American Enterprise*, January/February 2003.
3. Kathleen Klink, "Freeing the Student Press for Their Good and Ours," *School Administrator*, April 2002. www.aasa.org.
4. Kevin W. Saunders, "Should Children Have First Amendment Rights?" *Responsive Community*, Summer 2003, pp. 16–17.
5. Paul Rosenzweig, "The Ashcroft Legacy: Liberty and Security," *WebMemo #607*, Heritage Foundation, November 10, 2004. www.heritage.org.
6. Quoted in American Civil Liberties Union, "Freedom Under Fire: Dissent in Post-9/11 America," December 8, 2003. www.aclu.org.
7. Jonah Goldberg, "Speech Impediment," *National Review*, February 27, 2006.
8. Michael K. Powell, statement made at the Federal Communications Commission's 2002 Biennial Regulatory Review, www.mediaaccess.org.
9. Ron Paul, statement before the U.S. House of Representatives, March 10, 2004. www.lewrockwell.com.

Should Limits Be Placed on Free Speech?

10. Oliver Wendell Holmes, decision in *Schenck v. United States*, March 3, 1919. http://supreme.justia.com.
11. Frank Murphy, decision in *Chaplinksy v. New Hampshire*, March 9, 1942, http://supreme.justia.com.
12. David L. Hudson Jr., "Libel & Defamation," First Amendment Center, February 15, 2007. www.firstamendmentcenter.org.
13. Antonin Scalia, *R.A.V. v. City of St. Paul*, June 22, 1992. http://supct.law.cornell.edu.
14. Gerard Alexander, "Illiberal Europe," *On the Issues*, June 23, 2006, p. 4.
15. Richard Delgado, "Hate Cannot Be Tolerated," *USA Today*, March 2, 2004. www.usatoday.com.
16. Harvey Mansfield, "The Cost of Free Speech: In the Universities It's Almost as High as the Tuition," *Weekly Standard*, October 3, 2005, p. 39.
17. Potter Stewart, concurring opinion in *Jacobellis v. Ohio*, June 22, 1964. http://caselaw.lp.findlaw.com.
18. Phyllis Schlafly, "Supreme Court Sides with Pornographers Again," EagleForum.org, July 14, 2004. www.eagleforum.org.
19. Janet M. Larue and Kristina A. Bullock, "Brief of Amici Curiae, National Law Center for Children and Families, Concerned Women for America, National Coalition for the Protection of Children & Families, and Citizens for Community Values, in the Support of the United States, *et al.*, Appellants," January 10, 2003, p. 5. www.communityinterest.org.
20. William Rehnquist, decision in *U.S. v. American Library Association*, June 23, 2003, p. 15. http://supct.law.cornell.edu.

Should Speech Be Limited to Protect National Security?

21. Constitutional Rights Foundation, "Press Freedom vs. Military Censorship," January 11, 2006. www.crf-usa.org.

22. Nat Hentoff, quoted in Paul M. Weyrich, "Guarding the Home Front," *Reason*, December 2001. www.reason.com.

23. Jack D. Douglas, "None Dare Call It Censorship," November 29, 2005. www.lewrockwell.com.

24. Richard Posner, "Security Versus Civil Liberties," *Atlantic Monthly*, December 2001. www.theatlantic.com.

25. Christopher B. Daly, "Stop the Presses!" *Chicago Sun-Times*, May 21, 2006. http://findarticles.com.

26. Cal Thomas and Bob Beckel, "Protest Votes," *USA Today*, February 7, 2007. www.usatoday.com.

Should the Media Be Censored?

27. Motion Picture Production Code of 1930 (Hays Code). www.artsreformation.com.

28. Carrie Rickey, "A More Adult Way to Rate Movies for Kids," *Philadelphia Inquirer*, March 27, 2007. www.philly.com.

29. Rod Gustafson. "Ratings Versus Censorship," *Parenting and the Media*, Parents Television Council, October 2, 2003. www.parentstv.org.

30. Parents Television Council, "About Us," www.parentstv.org.

31. Federal Communications Commission, "In the Matter of Complaints Against Various Television Licenses Concerning Their February 1, 2004 Broadcast of the Super Bowl XXXVIII Halftime Show," February 21, 2006, www.fcc.gov.

32. PEN Center USA, "Censorship on Television: When Crying 'Indecency' Goes Too Far," February 18, 2005. www.penusa.org.

33. Joan Bowlen, "Whole Lot of Singing Never Gonna Be Heard," *Washington and the Arts*, March 1, 2007. http://tip-wm.net.

34. Jay Evensen, "Some Cartoon Images Override Political Point," *Deseret Morning News*, February 12, 2006. http://findarticles.com.

35. Quoted in Shannon Maughan, "Listservs Buzzing over Newberry Winner," *Publisher's Weekly*, Children's Bookshelf, February 15, 2007. www.publishersweekly.com.

36. David Hawpe, "In a Sex-Saturated Culture, Certain Body Parts Remain Unspeakable," *Louisville Courier-Journal*, March 7, 2007.

Are the Free Speech Limits in the Patriot Act Justified?

37. John Ashcroft, "The Terrorist Threat: Working Together to Protect America," prepared remarks at a Senate Judiciary Committee Hearing, March 4, 2003. www.usdoj.gov.

38. Paul Rosenzweig, "Securing Freedom and the Nation: Collecting Intelligence Under the Law," testimony before the U.S. House of Representatives Permanent Select Committee on Intelligence, April 9, 2003,www.heritage.org.

39. Alberto Gonzales, interview by Soledad O'Brien, "Gonzales: Speed an Issue in Secretive Wiretaps," CNN, December 19, 2005. www.cnn.com.

40. American Library Association, "Resolution on the USA Patriot Act and Related Measures That Infringe on the Rights of Library Users," January 29, 2003. www.ala.org.

41. John Ashcroft, speech delivered on

September 15, 2003 before the National Restaurant Association. www.usdoj.gov.

42. John Tirnan, "A Focus on Facts Ought to Dispel Mistrust of US Muslims," *Christian Science Monitor*, January 31, 2005.

43. Walt Brasch, "The Patriot Act and Free Speech: The Fiction Behind National Security," *CounterPunch*, March 7, 2002. www.counterpunch.org.

44. Tom Maertens, "Patriot Act Ineffective and Needlessly Tosses Aside Constitutional Protections," *St. Paul (MN) Pioneer Press*, August 19, 2004. www.commondreams.org.

List of Illustrations

List of Illustrations

Index